Accolades

2014 Poetry Collection

Published by
The America Library of Poetry
P.O. Box 978
Houlton, ME 04730
Website: www.libraryofpoetry.com
Email: generalinquiries@libraryofpoetry.com

Printed in the United States of America.

THE AMERICA
LIBRARY OF POETRY

ISBN: 978-0-9773662-9-3

Contents

Poetry by Division

Foreword

There are two kinds of writers in the world.
There are those who write from experience,
and those who write from imagination.
The experienced, offer words that are a reflection of their lives.
The triumphs they have enjoyed, the heartaches they have endured;
all the things that have made them who they are,
they graciously share with us, as a way of sharing themselves,
and in doing so, give us, as readers, someone to whom we may relate,
as well as fresh new perspectives
on what may be our common circumstances in life.
From the imaginative,
come all the wonderful things we have yet to experience;
from sights unseen, to sounds unheard.
They encourage us to explore the limitless possibilities
of our dreams and fantasies,
and aid us in escaping, if only temporarily,
the confines of reality and the rules of society.
To each, we owe a debt of gratitude;
and rightfully so, as each provides a service of equal importance.
Yet, without the other, neither can be truly beneficial.
For instance, one may succeed in accumulating a lifetime of experience,
only to consider it all to have been predictable and unfulfilling,
if denied the chance to chase a dream or two along the way.
Just as those whose imaginations run away with them never to return,
may find that without solid footing in the real world,
life in fantasyland is empty.
To our many readers, it is our hope that in the pages to follow,
you will find both heartfelt tales of experience,
and captivating adventures of imagination.
It is our pleasure to present them for your enjoyment.
To our many authors,
who so proudly represent the two kinds of writers in the world,
we dedicate this book, and offer our sincere thanks;
for now, possibly more than ever,
the world needs you both.

Paul Wilson Charles
Editor

Editor's Choice Award

The Editor's Choice Award is presented
to an author who demonstrates not only
the solid fundamentals of creative writing,
but also the ability to elicit an emotional response
or provide a thought provoking body of work
in a manner which is both clear and concise.

You will find "Home Alone"
by Brittany Loveless on page 217 of Accolades

2014
Spirit of Education
For Outstanding Participation

Cooper Junior
High School

Wylie,
Texas

Presented to participating students and faculty
in recognition of your commitment
to literary excellence.

Division I

Grades
3-5

Riverdance
by Reagan Beauregard

Feel that beat of Riverdance
The dance at the speed of lightning
Lightning that makes music
Those dancing feet of a story
Story of new changes
Changes of different cultures
The beat of dancing feet
Feet that bring a dance to life
Life that keeps the story going
Going as fast as you can dance
Dance is done and everything is still
Still as they are
They move off the stage
Off the stage, the crowd is cheering.

The Cat In the Polka Dot Hat
by Brooke Robbins

There once was a pretty orange cat
who just loved his polka dot hat
he won't play in the light
he doesn't like bright
so he sits in the dark on a mat

What I Do When There Is No School
by Olivia Maniskas

In the morning
I brush my teeth
Then I brush my hair
After I eat breakfast
Sometimes I go outside
Or I might play a board game
Sometimes I might make a craft
Or I might play with my sister
After I take my dogs for a walk
Then I eat dinner
Sometimes I go to soccer
When I get home I go to bed

Planting Flowers
by Noelle Collet

Dig holes in the ground
Then you put some seeds in them
Water and sun oh,
Watch your flowers grow so nice
Now you are done, wow good job!

The Grass Is Moving
by Tarun Emani

The grass is moving
It is tickling my small feet
The grass is moving
It's swaying across the ground
It is jumping up and down

Easter Is Coming
by Amanda Wildaver

Today is Easter
Easter eggs all over the yard
So much great candy
Chocolate, jellybeans and mints
Don't forget chocolate bunnies

Pearl
by Nick Riedy

I was walking on the street and on my way going
I saw something white and glowing.
I was going to twirl when I noticed it was a pearl.
I wouldn't give it to any girl.
Maybe I could sell it and buy something I could keep, maybe I'll buy a jeep.
I slipped on some ice, it wasn't very nice.
Mother of pearl I lost it, it must have been the squirrel.
It wasn't really worth but it must still be on earth.
Maybe I'll go home and look there.
When I got there I was in a stare.
I noticed right there was a girl with the pearl.

Spring
by Bryce Walsh

Sunshine
Bright light, mountains
Blocking, shining, blinding
The sight of the sun beautiful
Sunset

Lions' Den
by Rosabella Daraoui

I'm in a lions' den, praying that I'm rescued before the lions are awakened.
My prayers were answered, I was rescued
and Onoma was put to jail with a bang and a clatter.
My mom just finished telling me where she hid the gold,
when a man named Onoma stopped walking when he heard the word gold.
Mom sent me off to the quest. When my Mom couldn't see me anymore,
Onoma stopped me and told me if I don't tell him where the gold is,
He'll put me in a lions' den. I refused to tell him.
He threw me into a lions' den at night.
I'm in a lions' den praying that I'm rescued before the lions are awakened.

A Dark Day For Man
by Luc Greene

Zombie invasion
Run away so you don't die!
They come up from graves
We need to fight them
So they do not eat our brains
Board up the windows!
Chain or lock your door
So no zombies get inside
Or else you will die!
Try and get supplies
So you have a lot of stuff
To fight the zombies
Find some survivors
To help defeat the zombies
And get our world back!
The survivors died
Zombies are taking over
I am the last one.

Sunny
by Kiana Ahmari

I have a friend who is funny
Called "Sunny"
I always put my sunglasses on
To see my friends or friends all gone
Sunny and me are silly

Elasmosaurus
by Gabriel Angelo Webster

Sea monsters are big.
They like to eat fish and crab.
They are cool reptiles.

Bats
by Laura Barber

Bats suck while they chew.
Bats can suck animal's blood.
Baby bats are cute.

Through the Eagle's Eye
by Meagan Sherman

Through the eagle's eye you see,
the joyous bright free key.
That key you see is the freedom key
that shall earn your country's glee.
The glee you see are new free keys
in the doors that you will see.
When you earn those keys you open the
doors and you always see free glee.
You can find the last free key, then
you open the door to free.
That last door you see will lead you
to the eagle's eye. Through the
eagle's eye you see, the joyous
bright free key.

Giraffes
by Allison Wong

Giraffes are awesome
The giraffes frolic and dance
What a pretty sight!
How pretty they are
Rothschild is very rare
They have white stockings.
Giraffes are so smooth
When they cuddle together
When they sleep at night.
Calves are beautiful
Babies stumble towards their mom
They eat from bushes.
Calves stay near their mom
Moms protect their calves from harm
They travel in herds.
They aren't all the same
They all have different coats
I love all giraffes!

Sisters
by Payton Pugh

They're sweet, they're kind,
they'll never leave me behind.
They're loud, they're quiet,
they may cause a riot.
If I stumble and fall,
they'll help me stand tall.
Young or old,
they'll keep me warm when I'm cold.
When I'm scared at night,
they'll scare away the fright.
The love that they share
shows that they care.
Friends may come and go but,
sisters are always going to be there.
I love them all dearly
and I'll say this very clearly
I'm so thankful you're my sisters!

Spring
by Jason Wood

Flowers
Bloom, big
Planting, gardening, sprouting
Goes into a good smelling soil
Tulips

Maura
by Maura Dunn

There once was a girl named Maura.
That doesn't like Dora.
She never liked the show,
Now everyone knows,
and got hit with menorahs

The Cat With Big Ears
by Maya Kasim

There was a cat with big ears
who went to Sears.
His ears got caught in the door
and the people laughed and wanted more.
The cat in Sears
wanted to get rid of his ears.
The cat was brown
and wore a crown
to hide his ears
for many years.
All the dogs made fun of the cat
so he hid his ears in many hats.
Then one day
the cat went out to play.
The wind blew off his hats
and the dogs got scared of the cat.
The cat learned it is important to like yourself
and now he could leave all his hats on the shelf.

Take Your Time
by Oliver Mahoney

A day is a day so do what you can,
Go with the flow and don't fight against it,
Get it done but not in a rush,
Don't race time to the finish line.

Plants
by Natalia Rosser

Plants are cool to see.
Sugar pines can grow up tall.
I like seeing plants.

Dreams
by Kelsy Moschak

I used to be very crazy,
but now I am so very lazy.
All day I lie in bed.
Very often I fill my head,
with stories of very silly things,
of springs and tigers
and elephants on swings!

Going ... Going ... Gone
by Owen Fischl

I step up to the plate,
I'm not thinking about my date,
The pitcher is so boring,
So he is going to see that ball soaring,
And here's the pitch ... Whack!
That ball is over the wall,
And it's not going to fall,
As I'm rounding third base,
I fell and hit my face,
Wow, what a disgrace!
Even though that wasn't so great,
I got the last laugh when I crossed home plate.

How Animals Talk
by Adrian Davalos

Bumblebees are cool.
They give a lot of honey.
I love them a lot.

Spring
by Noah Thompson

Spring, spring here again
The long winter is over
let the rain begin

Summer
by Leah Hobbs

Oh summer, why aren't you here.
I need to go outside and play
in your hot summer breeze
and blow away the winter storms
so I can wear shorts again
and play in the green, green grass again.
Summer, oh summer, why aren't you here!
Oh please, come back to me!

Me and My Friends
by Gabrielle Schmidt

Me and my friends play all day but at night we meet for a surprise
No one ever knows the games, we play all day long
We also like animals a lot, we go to the zoo a lot too
We play with animals all day long
At 8:00 am and pm. We eat ice cream at lunch
We go to Friendly's and get ice cream so we would have ice cream
three times a day but it is all fun and games
When our dogs come running after us
but after running we take a swim in a lake or a pool
and we go to a baseball game when we can but if it is all full
we watch it on the TV.

Our Sense of Touching
by Afriyie Boakye-Yiadom

Some things will feel cold.
Some things will feel warm or hot.
Some things will feel cool.

Pets
by Primo Rode

Cat
Furry, lazy
Sleeping, pouncing, climbing
Claws, whiskers, rambunctious, guard
Playing, walking, whining
Friends, playful
Dog

Spring
by Kyler Adryan

Playing
Fastball, pitcher
Batting, throwing, catching
Hit then run the bases to home
Baseball

Beautiful Browns
by Gabrielle Greene

I am a beautiful brown. Can't you hear that beautiful sound?
It's the sound of love and hope which we believe in.
When I close my beautiful brown eyes, it's like I'm not even sleeping.
When I wake up with beautiful brown breath,
it might stink to you but to me it is called good rest.
I love my beautiful brown hair! Even when it's out and everywhere!
Those caramel streaks lighting it up. My skin can feel it brightening it up.
The way I walk makes me feel so brown and beautiful.
The others stare at me different, watching me walk the school narrow entrance.
When I am inside, the others tease me, but sooner or later they do leave me.

Weather
by Christian Otto

Weather is cool stuff.
Air has weight called air pressure.
Air is all around.

The Boxer
by Jake Chamberlain

Boxers are good pets.
Boxers are medium sized.
Boxers have short tails.

You Have a Frown
by Angela Sorbello

You have a frown.
What's got you down?
I'm here for you.
Isn't that true?
Was it an enemy?
You can tell me.
Please don't be mad.
You'll make me sad.
Was it a foe?
Or did someone you know go?

Friends
by Tatum Dolan

Everyone needs friends.
Friends stand side by side,
shoulder by shoulder, and boot by boot.
Your friend is the root, and you are the petals.
Together you are a flower and that creates girl power.
Share a headband, hold a hand, when feeling down
together make happy music with a great sound.
Happiness count and it starts
with making a friend.

Poor Girl
by Jolie Slobodin

My sister Jocelyn is a musician,
She also loves addition,
She once made a perfect rhyme,
All about time,
That strange girl ended up with a bad mental condition!

God Is Love
by Gabrielle Browne

God is love from Heaven above,
He always does right,
He's always good,
Even though He doesn't have to do it,
In our neighborhood.
We always sin,
But Jesus died on the cross for them.
We can change our hearts,
By listening to God.
He made our hearts,
With kindness,
And love.
As I said God is love,
Wherever we go.
He is the person I love to know.

Friendship
by Yasmine Oueslati

Friendship is great
Friendship is real, not fake
It does not matter what you look like or your weight
Because you're really great
With an awesome personality and phenomenal character traits
A friend will make each other laugh
We have sleepovers and other sorts of fun
We are against bullying yet we encourage each other to be strong
We will talk all day even if it's wrong
Sometimes it can be long
There are plenty of things we can do together
We can write a song and sing along

My Land
by Matias Amiel

I wish my land could fly across the sky
Nobody allowed to cry or lie
When you get off my land
You will get a big band
And you will be by far allowed to cry

France Dance
by Sarah Amtsberg

There once was a guy named France
Who wanted a new pair of pants
He sat in the tub
When he started to rub
He sat
and saw a bat
he hid in a barrel
with his friend Carol.
He found a nail.
Then he wanted to bail.
A guy named Bob
Who wanted a glob.
There was a huge boom.
And it was in my room.

Silver Blossom and Butterfly
by Aruna Balasubramanian

I was walking down the street,
When my feet just stopped to a halt!
It was very strange.
There was nothing within range!
My legs started walking,
To a place I've never seen,
And in a river, oh wow, oh my!
A silver blossom and butterfly!
They disappeared when I came too close,
Was it a mirage?
I don't know!
The only thing I know is that it was there.
And ever since I have silver-brown hair!

Pray
by Caden Boyer

I give to the poor, I pray for the sun,
I give a good greeting to everyone,
I hope that God likes me, the day that we meet
If only one chance to sit at his feet.
So when the world gets tough,
And life's going wrong,
I'll always remember ...
Heaven's where I belong!!!

What's Inside My Garage
by Logan Paczewski

Golf range
Golf balls
A lot of shelves
Gold clubs
My skis
And footballs

Bunnies
by Michele Park

Bunnies are soft
But sometimes they make
Me cough.
I love bunnies
So does Connie
They are warm
They are cute
But I think they're mute
Bunnies are awesome
Bunnies are ... wait you said to
Write about monkeys!?!
But they're not even
Monks or keys
They're monkeys!

Pigs
by Crystal Chang

Pigs, pigs,
Rolling in the mud
Pink and red like a rosebud
Eating anything
A bucket or two
They are adorable
And that is true

When You Play Soccer ...
by Megan Bertoti

When you play soccer you will always be running and moving
When you play soccer you can play in 4 positions,
goalie, offense, defense and midfield
When you play soccer you're always kicking the soccer ball
When you play soccer I guarantee you will have fun

Basketball
by Kai Childs

Basketball,
Is fun, mostly
Everyone plays it,
You can do lots of things
Like shoot, play defense, block,
Steal and dunk.

Narwhals
by Liam Carlin

What is that speeding through the sea?
It's a majestic narwhal and company
The gray creature fast and sleek
You have to admit, it's quite unique
Its horn is great and filled with pride
When it comes algae hides
And now that's all you need to know
So I really need to go.

Autumn Adventures
by Jacob Peifer

Bright colorful leaves,
Crunching when people come by,
Raking all the leaves,
Jumping into leaf piles,
Orange, yellow, red today

Laughs
by Annie Shin

Rumbles
Tumbles
Jumbles
Bumbles
Rolls
Tolls
Lolls
Strolls
Blooms
Zooms
Booms
Dooms
LAUGH

Snow
by Pavitra Chall

White, fluffy snowflakes are falling from the sky,
They're so beautiful, oh my!
The snowflakes make a white and soft blanket,
I wish I could preserve them in my beautiful trinket.
This morning, my dad took me skiing,
Soon after, hot and yummy cocoa we were drinking.
Then I went sledding with my friends,
I yearn for this fun to never end.
We build a snowman as big as we could,
When it was finished, it looked really good.
The snowman was so very high,
I thought it would soon touch the deep, blue sky.
When the weather gets warm, there will be no snow on the ground,
But I will wait for next winter, when snow will soon come around.

Earth
by Angelo Venezia

Big and full of life
Rotating on its axis
From the swimming fish
To the happy singing birds
Oh what a beautiful EARTH

Cows
by Brandon Collins

Black and white and go "moo"
Eat grass but not very new
They live on a farm
And show no harm
Some people say they're boring
And they do lots of destroying
They're really really funny
Nowhere near as soft as a bunny
Those are some reasons that I like cows
If you could see me I'd be taking some bows

I Am a Boy That's Curious and Adventurous
by Jérôme Gantz

I am a boy that's curious and adventurous
I wonder what the world will be when I'm older
I hear birds chirping
I see the world changing before my eyes
I want to have a happy and peaceful life
I am a boy that's curious and adventurous
I pretend that I'm strong and brave
I feel good when I help a friend
I touch the softness of my rabbit's fur
I worry that pollution will spread across the world
I cry when another tree is cut down
I am a boy that is curious and adventurous
I understand that people will be better than me
I say stop to bullying
I hope I will be a good leader when I grow up
I try to be nice with my friends
I dream that people will not be poor
I am a boy that is curious and adventurous

Spring
by Jason Profka

Nature
Bunnies, sunshine
Shining, hiking, camping
My favorite season of the year
Easter

Hummingbird In the Flowers
by Isabella Morales

The flowers in bloom lit up the whole afternoon,
And the sweet flower scent– up in the air it went.
And the lively colors reflected in the water,
Which made it very easy to spot her.

Surprise!
by Jordyn Sherry

"We are going to Disney World!" my parents told me one day,
I threw my arms around them yelling, "HOORAY!"
I was so excited I couldn't wait to go,
I packed up my bags faster than you would know!
The plane ride was long but we eventually got there,
It was so huge all I could do was gaze and stare!
To our grand hotel was the first place we went,
Then I paid for tickets, money well spent!
I used the tickets to get into the new place,
Once I stepped in I saw old Mickey's face!
The ride lines were long but I was patient enough,
Although that roller coaster ride was very rough!
Then we visited the race tracks and I drove a race car,
I drove it so very fast and I went so very far!
Back at the hotel we swam in the pool,
It was gigantic, warm and so very cool!
That very peaceful night we slept like soft and sound dogs,
Then we woke up and went on one more ride, a flume; in logs!
Soon it was the end, but at least I got a chocolate ice cream cone,
My trip to Disney was surely a blast, but we needed to head home.

The Dirty Car
by Noah Hill

The
Car is
So very dirty
Needs to be washed
Honk!

Keep Your Faith
by Dana Mejia

God gave us faith to keep us safe.
We pray in Jesus' name, for He has much grace.
He created a gate to save us at the end of time.
God will make everything fine even when you have lost your trust in faith.
Through joy or sorrow, you must never lose your faith.
For it will be a disgrace, God will save you even if you are angry, happy,
Or surprised with God, He will save you until the end of time.
God will always be with you because the Father Almighty will
Always love us so very much!

This Is Why I Read
by Nakeisha Martinez

Books, I love them.
They're portals to different lands,
they take you far and wide.
People ask why I read.
I ask them,
"Have you seen this beautiful thing?"
The story's short but excellent!
A story of kings and queens,
of knights and heroes,
of wizards and witches casting their spells,
of princes and princesses.
When we want to escape this world, we read,
we fall in love with great characters,
some make us smile, some cry,
some mysterious, some humorous, some give us facts.
They help us escape life and they stay in our hearts.
Books, I love them.
This is why I read.

A Cold Day
by Maisy Kellum

Wind
strong, cold
blowing, howling, swirling
nipping on my nose
breeze

The Friend Trend
by Ann Marie Saavedra

My friend is lazy 'cause she's CRAZY
She is smart and she likes pop tarts
She is TALL like the mall
She is creative but not that persuasive
She is WEIRD like my uncle's beard
She is nice as mice
She is funny but not like a bunny
It's okay 'cause we're all the same
We are human like Mrs. Dulin
We are 100% perfectly imperfect
I like my friend and hope that doesn't end.

The Time Is Drawing Near
by Nicholas Antolick

The time is drawing near, my son
For if yesterday is gone, what is today?
Make the most of today, my son
The time is drawing near
The time is drawing near, my son
For if today is now, what is tomorrow?
Make the most of today, my son
The time is drawing near
The time is drawing near, my son
For if tomorrow is not here yet, what is today?
Make the most of today, my son
The time is drawing near
The time is drawing near, my son
For if your life is gone, what are you?
Make the most of your life, my son
The time is drawing near

Success
by Arya Patel

I am a pearl hidden deep under the sea
and you have to be ready to achieve me.
Some basic steps are reading and writing
and always avoiding fighting.
Achieving me can earn you a lot of fame,
but you have to be ready to play this game.
Intelligence and focus leads the way
and laziness hates to see me stay.
Laziness and carelessness drive me away
and make the lazy people go on their bed and sleep for a day.
Courage and determination attract me
and those are the main key.
Set your goal and follow them strong
and never will you be wrong.
Always learn whenever you can
and be learning's #1 fan.
Becoming smart is the achievement for me
and success will never flee.
Yet, I am priceless to be sold,
but the secret of success is always told.

Sisters Forever
by Jahnavi Palarapu

Finally she was born, a cute adorable sis,
I knew she would need cuddles, hugs and of course a kiss.
Cuddly and warm, that's how she felt,
Her cute and adorable smile, made my heart melt.
First day at home, she slept and slept,
When she woke up, she wept and wept.
This is not how I had expected her to be,
Neither laughing or jumping or playing with me.
Then slowly she learned how to crawl, walk and run,
And that was when the real fun had begun.
Whatever I said, she would say it too,
Without even knowing if it was actually true.
Fighting however, was our worst problem yet,
We sometimes wished we had never met.
When one of us would get into a deep dark mess,
The other would help them get out of distress.
Even if we did something we said we would never,
We would still be sisters forever and ever!!

Fish On
by Davon Hein

I cast, I cast, I cast again.
I cast, I cast, I cast to the end.
I love fishing so much.
But it stinks when I don't catch a bunch.
I need to catch a bunch so for lunch I can munch, munch, munch.
It starts to drizzle.
I get a nibble.
I set the hook.
I get him in.
Now it's ready to cook.
So I tie on a new hook.

Free
by Marina Schnell

No homework left, no chores to do, so run!
Just spin under the sun!
Twirl until you fall down laughing in the cool grass!
Let the warm summer breeze trickle through your hair
like an airborne river.
And when the sun sets and fireflies light their tiny lanterns,
leap across the grass and catch one of those flying stars in your hand
and let it go.
And when you can see your feet no more,
twirl and leap, glide and run,
back through your front door.

The Pizza Hut
by Taylor Sherry

I went to a Pizza Hut, and guess what I saw.
A bear and a raccoon, eating twenty pizzas raw!
The pizza man came up to me, he was as tall as a wall,
Standing there so straight, standing there so tall!
The tall man said, "We are closed at night."
I was so scared, I had a chill of fright.
I will never come here, when it's closed at night,
Because if I do, I will leave with a fright.

The Starry Night
by Taylor Kay

The stars in the sky
They open your eyes to see
That they are something
They go twinkle in the night
It makes me think about what it could mean

Basketball
by Maureen Farrell

Running down the court
Pounding the ball down
Off your hand to the ground
You stop
Call out a play
It gets set
Up you go
In for the basket ...
You make it
Your teams goes
Crazy!

A Turtle's World
by Eliana Youssef

I am a turtle new to this land
I was born in a world surrounded by sand
I wandered away and ended up in a bog
Off in the distance I saw a green frog
I noticed around me things were so tall
I never realized I was so small
As time went by the familiar sounds were gone
Soon the night turned to the bright new dawn
It was sad to think I would see my family no more
To continue seemed like a humongous chore
The frog seemed to know why I was sad
And helped me to the water, it wasn't so bad

Milkshakes
by Sierra Frey

Chocolate, strawberry, vanilla
I like milkshakes
They are so sweet
They are my favorite treat
I ask and say please
Even though they give me a brain freeze
Doesn't everyone love milkshakes?

Dance!
by Madison Williams

One step, two step, three step, four
I like hip-hop and much more
Ballet, lyrical, jazz and more
Dance is meant for sure

Summertime
by Damien Ronca

Summer is starting
no more school
the weather is warm
time to swim in a pool
I pack my bags
and go to the shore
the beach and the boardwalk
I'm ready for more
I like to watch the Phillies play
I hope I get to go watch a game
amusement parks with lots of rides
and playing games to win a prize
there is just so much to do
this is why I love the summertime
when I am at home
during the day or at night
I like to play with my friends outside
I like to eat ice cream
out in the sun
summer is just so much fun.

Ann
by Brittany Lanning

There once was a girl named Ann,
She always dressed like a man,
She wore men's shoes,
She read the news,
Ann cooked eggs in a pan.

What Friends Do
by Manan Pancholy

Friends are loyal
Friends are true
Those are the things
That friends do
Friends are caring
Friends are kind
Even when
You're in a bind

Poems
by Anna Gerner

Long or short,
Big words or small words,
Write about anything and everything,
Words, poems made into songs,
Like The Star-Spangled Banner,
So many different kinds of poems,
Acrostic,
Cinquain,
Concrete,
Couplets,
Diamante,
Limericks,
Haiku,
Tanka,
I can't count how many kinds,
Rhyming or not rhyming,
Putting words in a paper,
I love words,
I love poems.

Beauty
by Kathleen Eisenhofer

The fool, some trailer carrying the foal.
All black, named Beauty.
The wheels going down the hard, bumpy road.
The black foal whinnied trying to get out.
There was no one to hear her, or save her.
The fool, some trailer was never seen again.
Neither the foal.
Not Beauty.
But if you look in the trailer
You will see the remainings of her horseshoes.
All red, dripping with ooze.
But not her.
Not Beauty.

Just a Dream
by Lauren Blick

As I awaken
I am shaken
I get up and stare
And see an unusual glare
Now I see
That the glare was meant to be
The bright and beautiful sun!
So I scream winter's done!
Let's go have some fun!
I run outside
And scream "Summer!" to hear worldwide
When they hear their jaws will be open wide
I stay out and play
In the wonderful warmth all day
Then I go to sleep
And start counting sheep
As I wake again
I realize that the warm sunny gleam
Was only just a little dream

A Dog At Your Door
by Alexis Paul

A dog at your door just waiting to be fed.
A dog at your door wanting some love.
A dog at your door needing a walk.
A dog at your door needing a bed.
You say, "What do you need? Hmmm ... a name!
I'll call you ... Buddy! Come here boy!"
My dog!

Birds
by Darielle Robinson

Birds,
Oh birds
With your
Small beak
That goes– tweet
Different colors
And long legs
Oh bird
You make me
Want to fly away

Spring Trampoline
by Jillian Loehr

In the spring
I go on the trampoline
I bounce so high
I can touch the sky
My feet are in a cloud
Look there's my house
I feel like a bird
It is so absurd
If I had wings
I would fly above the trees
I do not worry
I'm not in a hurry
I would smell the fresh air
And live my life without a care
I'm grinning from ear to ear
The sun is up and the sky is clear

Name
by Brianna Minnich

Brianna
It means funny, nice, friendly
It is the number 20
It is like a colorful rainbow
It is Florida
It is the memory of Popop
Who taught me patience and respect
It means to never give up and believe in yourself

Pie Or Cake
by Andrew Wilczewski

Pie
Yummy scrumptious
Eating baking sharing
Pie for pie people, cake for cake people
Enjoying combining gulping
Delicious sweet
Cake

Spring In the Air
by Judie Butler

Spring is in the air
Here and there and everywhere
The flowers start to sway
And the snow goes away
The weather gets warm
And the grass changes form
Days get longer
As the sun's heat gets stronger
Happy thoughts come to mind
As patches of snow become hard to find
And as rain starts to fall
Flowers open up like the greatest gift of all
But I think the best thing in spring
Is when everybody seems to sing
With joy and laughter
Knowing that there are many good things to come after

Opposites For a Fox and a Hedgehog
by Travis J. Williams

Fox
Fast skinny
Running eating interesting
One fast, one slow, which is found far away
Walking jumping sleeping
Plump prickly
Hedgehog

Autumn Is
by Grace Vigliotta

Tricky trick-or-treaters in creative costumes on Halloween night
Crisp, colorful leaves crunching under my feet on the cold cement
White, creamy whipped cream on top of the "perfect" pumpkin pie for dessert
The aroma of roasting Thanksgiving turkey in the oven
Sticky hands in the candy bowl
Autumn dances in leaves and they swirl around me as I play in my winter coat!

You Make Me Feel (hint: This Is a Song)
by Avery Noon

You make me feel
You make me feel
Like I was once
Like I was once
As happy as you
You make me feel
You make me feel
Like I was once
Like I was once
As happy as you
I felt all old and tired
I couldn't stand a chance
Until I met you darling
That all went away.
You make me feel
You make me feel
Like I was once
Like I was once
As happy as you

The Other Side
by Trevor Maranhaõ

My dear friend smiles down at me;
and it is plain to see;
I'm the one to blame;
and now time's end has come.
"No," my dear friend cries, but it is too late now,
I'm on the other side.

Frogs
by David Wolfe

Furless creatures
Rough slimy skin
Odd way of swimming
Green colored
Soaked by the muddy water

Spring
by Isabella Ferrara

Flowers are blooming.
No snow is shooting at me.
What a good day to be happy!
No one to bother.
Nothing to say.
Just to be happy on this wonderful day.
Spring break is coming.
Time to go.
Come on.
Let's go!
I get to relax.
In a nice warm bed.
When we come out, we find the eggs.
With candy and money.
I go out with my family.
For breakfast and fun.
I can't wait till next year.
The fun has just begun!

Vivid Peacock
by Shannon Taylor

White stripes border his watchful black eyes.
As he spreads his feathers out,
this black and blue dull-like body comes down to his feet.
His tall feathers show spots of green, orange, blue and black.
Creating his beautiful body.
The feathers stretch up from his head as he shimmers with the sun.
But if you get too close, he runs in fear from the humans,
screaming, howling and chirping
as you can really see his white curved beak.
As the sun sets it is time for the peacock and me to leave.
But when I come home, I can't stop thinking about
the time I had a chance to see a vividly colored peacock.

Welcome Summer
by Claire Kiester

Welcome
crashing waves
steaming sand
chirping chicks
cool ice cream
blooming flowers
Bienvenido
fresh fruit
beach volleyball
green grass
rumbling thunder
little ladybugs
Accueil
fast swimming
tall sunflowers
rushing rivers
swaying hammock
blue waters
Benvenuto
salty watermelon
pink starfish
no school
busy bees
shining sun
Welcome summer, I hope you last long!

Spring
by Miriam Alex

When the sun shows a ray of light,
And when the frosty mornings become so bright,
After the cold winter is gone, what do I hear?
The sweet chirping of birds because spring is near.
When the scent of flowers wafts through the air,
The smell of spring is everywhere.
At this time birds are hatched from oval eggs.
For all winter long it was warmed by its mother's legs.
Buds appear on the sturdy trees.
Sometimes I feel the cool spring breeze.
What exciting adventures in spring await?
Whatever it is, spring sure is great!

Music and Tunes
by Sandra Quintana

Music
Lyrical, melodical
Inspiring, singing, harmonizing
Songs, singers, bands, albums
Listening, dancing, performing
Upbeat, slow
Tunes

A Sore Throat
by April Chronowski

Good-bye dear voice,
I bid thee farewell.
Though I have found another voice
That will be just as swell.
This voice goes high,
This voice goes low.
And this voice doesn't crack quite so.
And I shall tell you this voice so you know,
This voice,
new voice,
is my cello.

My Mom
by Cheyenne Phelps

Mom is always there to help.
When I go down she picks me up.
Mom taught me many things
How to play my clarinet
When I crashed my car, she was there to help.
We do a lot of things together,
The things we do for life.
The things she has taught me,
Are the things I will need for life.
Like how to work and play,
How to be a sister and daughter.
My mom is one of those moms,
That teach their kids to be what they can.
I want to be just like her.
My mom says that I should be like her.

Summer
by Aidan Connor

We're out of school it's time to play
It feels like summertime
I will go play with my friends
and we can play sports
The flowers are growing

Most Dreams
by Bella Natale

Most dreams start with
little adventures.
Some are small,
like a bouncing ball.
Some are big,
like a giant pig.
Look at the time
it is time to rhyme.
See that tree
it is as tall as me.
Time to dream.
I hope my help
gave you a dream about kelp.

Oh, Mr. Pig
by Delaney Harty

Oh Mr. Pig, oh Mr. Pig,
Won't you play with me?
We could climb a mountain,
Or just a simple tree.
We could take a little swim,
In the swimming pool.
Or we could wear sunglasses,
And say that we are cool.
Oh Mr. Pig, oh Mr. Pig,
Right now I have to leave.
But maybe I could take you home,
With a ho and heave.

Spring, Spring
by Vivian Wu

Spring, spring adventure
Warm sunshine against my back
Baking up with sweat

A Furry Friend
by Rachel Lewiski

Furry, fuzzy, fantastic, friend
I hope our friendship will never end.
Time just flies when you're around,
And it seems as though no one but us makes a sound.
Mack, you are hereby crowned,
M.V.D. (Most Valuable Dog)

Summertime
by Connor Ludwig

School's out, time to have fun
Hanging with your friends, best time ever
Going to the pool, jump in, splash
Run through the sprinklers
Playing baseball, winning championships
Playing with your friends is so fun

The Beach
by Dahlia Whitcomb

At the beach it is very hot,
You see the people and there is a lot.
I want to be in the water all day,
But my sister likes to stay in the sand and play.
The girls liked to get tanned,
While they lay in the sand.
The sand gets wet by the waves,
So the crabs hide in very small rock caves.
As the sun starts to go down,
The people go home into town.

Diamonds
by Anthony Torres

Dazzling
In crystal-like appearance
Above all gems
My favorite mineral
Over beautiful
Never easy to find
Dynamic sight
Sparkling

Me, Myself, and I
by Madelyn Hannah

Madelyn
Who is adventurous, creative, musical, and smart
Daughter of Roddy and Amy; sister of Mark
Lover of her brother and her teacher
Who fears insects and spiders
Who needs friends and family
Giver of backpacks to homeless and presents to family
Who would like to see Paris, France and a show on Broadway
Resident of Pennsylvania
Hannah

Joshua
by Jay Grover

Joyful, good friend
Out of this world
Super kind
Helpful
Understanding
Always there for me

Friends
by Olivia Colwell

Friends bring joy
Real friends never judge you
Intelligent friends, crazy friends
Everlasting friends
Never forget your friends
Dumb friends or smart ones it doesn't matter
Simple friends come easy

Spring/Summer
by Kevin Wilkinson

Days I wait for warmth to come back
it's like spring is going too slack,
snow and snow is all I see
I guess I have to go and flee,
White is the horrible color
it is even annoying my mother,
school and school every day
I can't wait for the month of May,
that is when the weather is warm
also when my clothes are torn,
summer, summer, I can't wait
time to hang with the brother,
vacation time in July, time to go to the beach
enough with speech after speech,
in the pool every day
isn't that so cool,
time with friends to have some fun
in the very hot sun,
we can go to Dairy Queen
but only one can dream

My Cat
by Marissa Sharer

Meows when she is hungry
I love to tickle her stomach
Lays around the house and sleeps
Outdoor cat likes to hunt

Pokémon
by Mark Robertson

Pikachu has little red cheeks
Oshawott is an otter Pokémon
Koffing evolves into Weezing
Ekans evolves into Arbok
Magcargo is a snail Pokémon
Oshawott uses water pledge and bubble
Ninetales has nine tails

Fantastic Teachers
by Destiny Posaski

Fall open house is awesome!
Are you a good person, student, or teacher?
Nice kids are best.
The best teacher is the funniest.
All students should follow school rules.
Spell words correctly on essays.
Teach your brothers and sisters what you have learned in school.
It is fun when there is NO homework!
Choose your desk wisely.

Teachers help you understand topics better.
Every second counts.
Always follow the Dress Code.
Caring is a good character trait to have.
Help each other.
Each teacher helps in some way.
Read every day, it's good for you.
Study hard for tests and quizzes.

Spring
by William Bartusis

Summer is coming
Pigs are oinking
Rabbits are hopping
It is time for flowers
No more snow, more flowers
Green grass growing in the breeze

Imagination
by Sarah Anne Mash

Guiding my hopes and dreams,
Floating among the clouds,
Taking me to the stars and beyond,
Way above my worries and fears.
I float along lightly and carefree,
Nothing can harm me in my playground above the stars,
I feel safe to think about uncommon things,
Like journeys through forbidden mystical forests.
There are no judgments in my land,
Creativity and acceptance roam free.
In my imagination!

Spring Day
by Nora Idler

Birds wake me in the morning,
Warm sun on my face,
Burst of colors like a rainbow,
Grass waving in the wind,
Bees buzzing around,
I'm rolling in the grass,
Flowers smell sweet,
Peepers' chirps keep me up at night,
My senses come alive on this spring day.

Pencil and Eraser: Partners In Crime
by Zachary Cassidy

A pencil is like a burglar
>   sh, sh, sh.

it steals words from your mind
An eraser covers up its tracks
>   brush, brush, brush.

Footprints you must find.
While reading you write down clues
>   kc, kc, kc.

to know what crime they committed.
But you must read carefully to know
>   squint, squint, squint.

where signs have permitted.
You must hear which note they're sending.
>   strum, strum, strum.

They are so very tricky.
Sometimes it's a good crime, a happy ending.
>   ha ha ha

Though a sad ending really is a pity.
>   sigh, sigh, sigh.

My Cat Is Fluffy
by Raigan Lindholm

My cat is very fluffy, Fluffy is not her name.
Don't try to pet her, she has a furry mane
Her fur is very fluffy, but Fluffy is not her name.
If she hits me with her tail, I don't feel a thing
Because her tail is fluffy, it's not like a ring.
Her fur is very gray, black and white too.
If she falls in a pool her fur will turn black and blue.
If you shave her fluffy fur, and make it into a sweater,
You'd have two hundred of them, that's a lot better.
She has a lot of fluffy fur, I can't get in the house,
The only thing that can get in there is a tiny little mouse.
We once tried to shave her very fluffy fur,
It did not work for us, it was again, a very big blur.
Everyone now thinks her name is Fluffy.
Don't say that to her, you will get a little puffy.
My cat's fur is very soft like freshly homemade silk
Please I beg you, don't go by my cat's milk
I now you have not seen my cat but she is truly fluffy
And I know you won't bug her while she's watching Buffy.
I know you don't know her name, I will tell you, it's Puffy.

3rd Place

Mary Esposito

My Heavenly Mother
by Mary Esposito

The sun
Waves her dancing limbs
Sheltering my planet
And showering warmth
Upon the frigid corners
Of the world.
I bask in her glory
Absorbing her presence
Observing her radiance
Like an angel from Heaven.
The sun lifts me up
And cradles me in
Her rays of hope and light.
My heavenly mother
Always watching over me
In her golden kingdom bright.

2nd
Place

Linnea Geenen

Rain
by Linnea Geenen

Tapping against the glass,
tears fall from the sky,
as a river of sadness overflows.
The clouds cannot contain their sorrow.
Blanketing the world in darkness,
the sky lights up,
as screams echo through the air.
Dark gray turns to black.
Anger bursts forth,
as the clouds breathe out,
loud as a lion's roar.
The storm goes on.
The screaming softens,
to a moan,
and tears flow out again.
There is one last sniff ...
Then silence.

1st Place

Bridgette Rupp

One of the youngest authors in our contest this year
is also one of our most talented,
treating us to a beautifully descriptive poem about horses.
Bridgette entered as a third grade student who,
in addition to writing creatively,
likes to read, dance, and play softball.
She also enjoys swimming and spending time
with friends, family, and especially her chocolate lab, Sam.

Horses
by Bridgette Rupp

Ebony,
cream,
chestnut,
and caramel streaks
race across the immense beach,
scattering sand behind them,
galloping with the wind,
spreading across the sand in the open, empty night.
Only the sound of hooves against the warm earth
in the humid, summer night
fills the air around
the sweaty beasts.

Division II

Grades

6-7

Anne Frank
by Morgan Finney

The Gestapo, running through the town.
Are they looking for me?
"Adolf Hitler will disappear soon," I think.
"All Concentration Camps will disappear," I think.
Will all Jews disappear soon?
Later we sneak, running and hiding.
Will we survive?
Then, the monster, Adolf Hitler, is in front of me.
"Off to Auschwitz!" he says.
There is my mother, lying dead.
To Bergen-Belson here I come.
There lies my sister, as dead as my mother.
Oh why, oh why did this have to happen?
My friend throws me my last piece of bread, for sickness has come upon me.
I think of my family.
Then, I take my last breath.
For Adolf Hitler has won over my body, but my story will live on forever.
- Inspired by Anne's life and how she was forced to live it.

My Dog
by Matthew Burns

My dog is like Satan,
Eyes with a devilish look,
With dreams of catching a rabbit,
She's quite the devilish crook.
With legs just like sticks,
And the speed of a cheetah,
She runs just like Usain,
Which I think is insane.
She will steal your food,
If she's in the right mood,
She will not play fetch,
Unless the objects to fetch,
Have a heart and a pulse.
All these traits are so true,
So you better beware,
That ready to pounce,
She might sneak up on you ...
Righty there!

I Spy View
by Mary Elisabeth Hoffmann

I spy a hat, a cat, a mat,
A very large cow, and a dog named Splat;
A thumbtack, a humpback;
And don't forget a big map

A Spring Horse Farm
by Brigitte Lubker

A place of soft vibrant green grass sprinkled with dandelions
Fences, splintery, rustic, rattling
As the winds make it sway
And horses of dark chestnut to snow white
Carrying faint scents of leather off of weather worn saddles
Constant thump, thump, thump
Of hooves on training ring sand
With riders as straight as sticks
Lazy cats meander through dusty horse trails
Tastes of musty hay
Drift through a gentle spring breeze
Trails feel soft underfoot, soft as beach sand
Leading to a great brown faded barn
Golden light seeping through roof cracks
The milky perfume of soap whisks through the air
As riders prepare for the show.

Bullies
by Abigail Pfeiffer

Being bullied is something no one likes, sadly it happens everyday.
I see it in school, and all around, I wish it would all go away.
I know what those victims are going through, because I was bullied once too,
It really made me insecure, and for a while I was sad and blue.
Then finally one day I had enough, and stood up to the bully, though it was tough,
But with courage and strength, I had no fear, and told the bully,
STOP RIGHT HERE!
Ever since then I felt brave and confident too,
If I can stand up to my bully, I promise, so can you!

Past Life
by Jeremy Simon

Have you ever thought about your past life?
I have.
I know what I was, but do you?
Go find out!
Go ... go ahead.
It will amaze you.
You might be the person who made the first house.
You might be the smartest person in the world ... Who knows?
You will!

Easter Morning
by Alexis Ganzel

On Easter morning there was a lot of joy
Enjoy a wonderful summer
And brings a lot of toys
Easter duck and Easter chick,
Easter eggs with chocolate so thick.
Easter Bunny's very quick
Easter hats for one and all,
Easter ball bounces high
Easter Bunny makes a call!
Happy Easter always brings
Such a lot of pleasant things

A Skiing Trip That Went All Wrong
by Appalachia Kunz

I went skiing one day at Cannon
It was such a fun day we were planning
It was snowy and cold
And windy and white
And the trail we went on was such a beautiful sight
There was snow in my hair
And ice everywhere
And I slid on a bump and flew through the air
A bruise, a scratch and even a cut
But the worst I think ... was my broken butt

Scuba Diving
by Erek Bickford

My family and I were on a boat
Putting on our masks and flippers for scuba diving
I hoped that when I jumped I would float
Then, splash! I leaped off the boat
And I do not mean to gloat
But it was very fun splashing in the water
Diving down with sea otters
Swimming with the schools of sea fish
Looking at seaweed that seem to be waving at me
And I am betting that sometime you will wish
That you were scuba diving here in the deep blue sea!

Phillies Game
by Megan Dignam

It's the bottom of the 9th; Chase Utley is up to bat.
The pitcher is wearing his lucky baseball hat.
The score is 5-5, tie game,
Whoever wins gets all the fame.
He pitches the ball, and Chase Utley hits it.
The ball doesn't go in anyone's mitt.
It is traveling far,
It is as high as any star.
Chase Utley hit a home run,
The other team isn't having so much fun.

Rainbow of Personality
by Brigid O'Neill

Red is how you love, care, and share.
Orange is how you think, your thoughts compare.
Yellow is how you shine with your talents so brightly.
Green is when you pay attention rightly.
Blue is for the sorrow when things happen terribly.
Indigo is for the sincerity towards your friends and family.
Violet is the special "You", that makes people happy, too!
Rainbows can be your personality,
Each color is a different stage.
It does not matter what your age.

My Dog
by Mikayla Brown

My dog is the color of sand,
I love to hold her in my hands,
She's always playing outside,
She doesn't like to hide,
a very fast runner is what she is,
I bet you can't ace her quiz,
her tail is like a little stub,
oh and she's a chubby, chub, chub.
She's soft like a feather bed,
and she's very smart in her head,
she is wild like a chimpanzee,
but she loves me,
always quick on her feet,
especially when she's going to eat,
she has curly hair,
but she doesn't care.

Nothing But Net
by Zachary Dudley

Nothing but Net
Time ticking down
Cheerleaders and fans cheering
One minute left
Parker dribbling down the court
Passes to Duncan and ...
Bam! Slam dunk!
He went so high he was like a bird
Soaring through the sky
LeBron gets the ball and the three
Spurs get the ball
Parker tries a jumper
Blocked by Bosh
LeBron tries the three and
Misses
Bosh gets the rebound
Dishes it out to Allen
3, 2, 1
Swish
Nothing but net

Courage
by Nathaniel Perrins

The gut feeling gives you butterflies
It's all up to you
Win or lose
Which takes a lot of courage to do

Love
by Katlyn Davis

Be with the one that makes you happy,
The one that makes you smile,
The one that makes you laugh,
And every day worthwhile,
Live life for the moment,
Try hard to make it last,
Because life is so short,
It goes by so fast,
So when you find love,
Don't let it slip away,
Hold it forever,
And cherish it each day,
As long as you are happy,
That is what you should do,
Love that someone and let them know,
Before your life is through.

Give It Your Best
by Jenna Smith

Never give up,
Try your best,
Try, try to fly.
You may have some falls,
One or two,
But don't give up you.
See your dreams,
Let them be free.
Don't give up on what you need to achieve.
Stay strong and fight,
You might be surprised by what you can do,
If you just believe in "You".

Someday
by Lauren Stepniak

Someday I will dance like a snowflake twirling in the air
Someday I will run; like a fawn in a field
Someday I will sing like a robin with no care
Someday I will use my hands to paint a moonbeam
Someday I will be whatever I dream

Fever
by Sara Flynn

I am an empty city
If not dead
Everyone has fled,
Sickness lingers between my streets and alleys
Five thousand dead and only more to come
I am an empty city
No wants to come near me
I used to thrive and be healthy
But now fever has taken over me
Thieves on every street
Wailing from every block
I am an empty city
Lonely, deserted and feared by all.
Yellow is everywhere
On doorknockers, poles and windows
But mainly in people's eyes
I used to be thriving Philadelphia, but now
I am the empty city.

Courage
by Tyler Perkins

Courage is to be brave
Stand up and do something others won't
It is also to be helpful and kind to one another
For an example
Being a firefighter and saving a person in the burning home
Another example
Being a policeman and taking out a robber with a gun
But courage is not always good
That robber had courage for doing a dangerous risk

The Circus
by Skylar Seeley

Filled with loud BANGS! And WHOOPS!
Lions jumping through blazing hoops.
Acrobats flying through the air and landing in poses,
Seals balancing balls on their noses.
Eating way too much buttery popcorn and cotton candy too,
And the only thing that could make it better would be if you were here too.

The Smallest Bird
by Emma Burke

Bright blue feathers spread
As the flock climbs that invisible sky stairs into
The air,
And travel among the bright autumn trees,
Letting the breezes tell them where they will go next.
They land, a great tree now beneath their small feet.
Their voices rise together, echoing among the trees.
But one bird,
Its small shape making the others look like eagles,
Sings louder.
Greater.
A small song rings out among a forest of giants,
And for a moment, the world revolves around it.
The smallest bird's heart had the loudest song.

Musings On a Day Like Today
by Neal Tinaikar

A soft, white blanket of snow gently piles up on the streets,
with the sun's piercing rays dashing through the sky.
Children play outside with wooden sleds,
and they build smooth ramps so they can fly.
A deer prances around a forest,
showing its gleaming, white and brown fur.
A rabbit bounces around a pogo stick,
but rapidly hops away in a blur.
I get out of my fluffy, soft, and cozy bed,
When I hear my mom asking what I am doing–
"Getting ready for school!" I say,
But I feel pretty dumb because just then I realize,
That today is a great, AWESOME snow day!

Pure Happiness
by Grace Toner

Cheer is a light that suddenly
Comes peeking out from a storm cloud.
Practice makes me feel relief from a long
Tiring day of school every time is a
Constant "hooray!"
Getting a jump, flip, or stunt right is like getting
And A+ on your overall grade
In all subjects letting pride rush through your fingertips.
Even when we drop a stunt or mess up
On our routine, we talk about
What we did wrong and fix it
Because we are a family.
So, as you can tell cheer to me isn't fake peppy girls,
It's pure happiness.

Dominick the Atomic
by Jonathan Sadanaga

Who is the most Atomic? Why Dominick,
The most Atomic Dominick of all Dominicks!
He knows all the Periodic Table,
Atomic Mass, number and Label,
For he's the REAL junior Einstein,
And as good at writing formulas as Doctor Victor Frankenstein!
Dominick is so obsessed with all his nonsense he shows us,
Like his tungsten carved sleek rhinoceros,
Merchandise of Fluorine DNA phosphorus,
And so much more– can you believe this preposterousness?
Well we can consider his brain a very powerful weapon,
Reading objects falling to the Earth at 9.8 meters per second per second,
So with this we can infer his brain is his central mass,
For it's so colossal big, and runs pretty darn fast.
So we're about to finish this poem on the most intelligent person
Who has ever existed,
Einstein, Tesla, Newton– Dominick easily tops the people I just listed.
Because only Dominick is the most atomic.
… So please explain how he's failing chemistry this semester.

Beach Day
by Kacey Coyle

Ahhh ... the beach! Such a nice place to be right now.
The sand is such a pretty color. It's like I'm stepping in muffin mix
as the shells act like mini chocolate chips.
The sand feels so hot against my feet. Every once in a while,
my foot hits a shell and it feels like a peach bud.
Everywhere I look, there are Coronado dunes surrounding me,
making me feel trapped at this beautiful place.

The Rough Seas
by Brina Cartagenova

Lift the anchor
Sail the seas
Through the tormenting ocean
Without a compass
Without a way
Cannot deceive the ocean
No way to steer
No way to turn
Through the endless motion
I've found no way
To live my life
I'm lost in the commotion

Baseball
by Ryan Bolli

As I wait for spring,
I think of the season it brings.
Baseball ...
The smell of freshly cut grass
and the bright warm sun on my face.
When I see baseball fields being prepped for the season,
I can hear the fans' loud cheering.
The best part of baseball is hearing the bat hit the ball.
Sitting on the bench enjoying the game with my teammates,
Cracking sunflower seeds and drinking ice cold water
is what I miss most of all.

The Talking Tree
by Kaci Deane

He was standing there
On a bright sunny day.
He saw a green tree
And let out a "Hey"
The tree said "Hi"
And the boy got scared.
So, he replied with a "Bye"
When the tree just glared.
The boy went back to the tree.
He lay against it's trunk.
They decide to make a treaty.
Then he sat there like a hunk.
The talking tree and boy became friends.
They saw each other every day.
They stayed together until the end.
They loved each other each and every way.

The Final Point
by Marley Turbett

The clock is ticking down,
you have turned this game around.
Then you rebound the ball,
and then you hear a call.
You take your hand and put it over your head,
and you throw the ball to whom your name was said.
The team has already set up in zone defense,
the clock's ticking down, and now you start to get tense.
4, 3, 2,
then the ball gets passed to you,
and then you glance at the clock and it is still tied up
then you throw the ball without even looking up.
The ball goes flying, and the buzzer goes off
at least if it didn't go in, you played very tough.
Then the ball goes in with a swish,
the winning point, everyone's wish.
The crowd starts to cheer, and goes in an uproar,
the game is over, and you are very sore.
It was all worth it– this 4 hour trip,
and the outcome was wining the state championship.

Bad Day
by Vincent Rudderow

Don't look at me, just leave me alone.
I'm not in the mood, so don't talk to me at all.
Just stop, alright, I don't want to fight.
Oh man, this day has been terrible, like you would care at all.
Maybe tomorrow will be a great day, unlike today.

The Painted Sunrise
by Ciara Smith

While the "Indian Paint Brush" paints the sky
A "Kumquat" is used to make the color of the sun
An "Orange Burst" runs along the horizon
The "Desert Sunrise" fills the atmosphere

Winter
by Kaity Sweeney

On a cold winter day,
When it feels too cold to play
And the snow blankets the town
And the falling ice makes a big sound
When the wind stings your nose
And bites at your toes
And the flames in the fireplace seem to dance
And the snowflakes almost appear to prance
On a cold winter day
When it feels too cold to play
The snow is as white as a cloud
And not a speck of grass can be found
When eating snow gives you a brain freeze
And the seasonal flu makes you sneeze
When shoveling your driveway is so bad
And all the potholes make drivers mad
On a cold winter day
When it feels too cold to play
But, we bundle up
And go out anyway

Into the Dimension
by Armando Petraccia

As I look into the portal,
I forget I'm a mortal.
The spiral of different colors
Looks like another world,
But as I'm hurled into a peculiar dimension
I wonder if I will get attention.
I'm an outcast on Earth,
But will I belong?

Coyotes
by Sarah Marple

Young, beautiful creatures of nature
Can be capable of anything
Adaptable they are.
Pain they fear,
stress they hold.
Always under pressure that someone is going to blow up their humble home.
Wonderful questioned animals from above.
They take innocent animals for themselves and their family.
Coyotes,
The amazing majestic wonder.

The Big Test
by Skylar Miller

There's a big test tomorrow
and I really need to study
"Go away Marvin, I don't need a study buddy!"
I'm frustrated and tired
I want to go to bed
I think I feel a fire, starting in my head!
2+2 is 4, and 5+5 is, wait!
I don't need to study math, I'm already doing great
Washington sailed the ocean, in 1492
Oh wait, that was Columbus, who sailed the ocean blue
A noun is an action, and a verb is a person, place or thing
I really need to study, before I start failing!

Oranges
by John Huttick

So juicy,
So sweet,
So good to eat.
Not spicy,
Not salty,
Not hairy at all.
Not crispy,
Not sharp,
Just smooth to all.
It's not creamy,
Not milky,
Not inky at all.
It's just orange,
And silky,
And the best
Thing for all.

Lucky Ones
by Lauren Benz

And if you consider yourself a candle;
lighting up the room with its "coral gold" flame then you are lucky
because most of us have burned out leaving only a dark room
and reminiscing thoughts of what used to be a "crushed orange" glow.
And if you consider yourself a star;
burning brightly with its "poppy gold" flames then you are lucky
because most of us are falling from the sky
fading from the "orange spice" color into the blackness of the lonely universe.

Walking In Hazel Woods
by India Barnes

I took a trip exploring in Hazel Woods.
Looking at the beautiful green Island Palm trees.
Smelling the Wethersfield Moss on the bottom of every tree truck.
Glancing up, down, and all around.
Feeling like I am in a Medieval Forest with all this green around me.
Green trees, green fog, green moss, green everything.
This adventure in Hazel Woods can be a trip bursting and
exploding with new life.

The Lonely Mountain
by Kieran Murray

Taller than trees
but doesn't grow.
Has a shadow
but no one shows.
You hear a voice but it's just the howling wind.
Slipping on ice
when you walk.
Look around for edges before you fall.
Do not enter caverns or caves.
Frost bite.
finally caught up to you.
You start feeling sick.
Then your legs and hands feel like rocks.
You find an edge
tempted to jump.
But you keep moving.
You see a light.
You made it to the top.

Only Human
by Alexandra Battisti

Never again will I see the "Modestly Peach" color of springtime flowers
waving in the wind
No more of that beautiful sunset color of "Candy Mix"
that brings tears to my eyes
Gone are the days on the beach, snorkeling in the water to find that one fish
the pretty color of "Coral Expression"
But what I will miss most of all is life itself,
With the flavor of "Daredevil" red raspberries exploding on my tongue
The sun in the sky, the ocean and the way we all splash around in it.
Though it's better this way, I guess.
I should just give in to the music lulling me to eternal sleep.
After all, I'm only human, I won't live forever.
And with a final smile and a look at the world, I let the life drain out of me.
It felt good, better than life itself.
After all, I'm only human.

Moving Day
by Gina Mullen

I was ten when my family bought a new house
"We move on July 11," my parents had said
The last day of school, I bid farewell to my friends with tear-stained cheeks
July 11 we packed up and left
"We move on July 11," my parents had said
Staring blankly out the car window through thick tears
July 11 we packed up and left
My heart sinking deep in my stomach
Staring blankly out the car window through thick tears
Memories of friends and schoolmates rushing through my head
My heart sinking deep in my stomach
Constant thoughts of my old life
Memories of friends and schoolmates rushing through my head
The last day of school I bid farewell to my friends with tear-stained cheeks
Constant thoughts of my old life
I was ten when my family bought a new house

Bon Voyage
by Maggie Wetzel

Life is riding a boat.
Swaying in a chilling darkness,
Soaring in a summer's light.
This boat doesn't stop,
Instead it is in a pursuit of happiness.
Along the way, boats crash, pass, and fall behind,
But your boat must continue to sail forward.
The boat drops anchors,
Slowing, pulling, and wishing for it to stop,
But it does not.
The boat must keep moving,
Never giving into the temptation to sink.
Everyone has a boat.
Everyone sways, soars, and in the end sinks.
This is not a controllable force,
All good things must come to an end.
The boat, in age, sickness, destruction, or whatever the cause may be,
comes to a stop.
It sinks.
Life is riding a boat.

My Dog
by Michaelia Kelley

I walk through the mahogany door to get my purple lunch box,
when to my surprise a little fluffy puppy wagging her tail 'round and 'round
stood before me.
Her small high pitched bark made my heart melt,
and her fur was as soft as cotton.
Cotton ... the sweetest name for the perfect puppy.
"Cotton!" I called, she seemed to know it as if she had heard it her whole life,
and she has known it ever since.

New Awareness
by Jake Rudloff

I am a person with more than I know
Not too far away there be people that lie
All day
Not too far away
Lies a man
Frozen to the bone
Wondering when he will eat
And where he will get it
I wonder why he doesn't get help
It's so bad and sad

The Game
by Melissa Flood

I dribbled down the court.
My heart is pounding.
I get to the 3 point line.
Time is running out.
I shoot
and when the ball goes in the net
it makes a swoosh sound.
The crowd goes wild.
Now it's a tie game.
We all are frozen in time.
We get the ball back.
We score.

Summer Starts Today
by Chloé Millett

I woke up to the soft sound of a bird
And headed out to the garden
The cran-apple colored roses were glowing in the sun
Summer has begun
I picked up the sweet spiceberry glass
And took a sip of the lemonade
As I looked out to the pier, I whispered
Summer is here
I swam into the crystal waters
And found a rose sachet jewel
My eyes were stunned at the sight
Summer has taken flight
I watched the sunset from my beach chair
And felt the waves lightly tap my feet
The rhubarb sky seemed to smile at me and say
Summer starts today

Tests
by Maria DiGiovanni

I begin my test.
I launch on a voyage
Upon a sea of knowledge,
Memory and challenge.
I sail through multiple choice questions,
Float over vocabulary,
And glide by reading comprehension.
I merge from the great waves
Of essay questions,
Applying my education and ability
To the most complex
Of quizzical questions
That are swimming before my eyes.
I end my travels
At the dock of relief and comfort.
I must always remember to study
Or I may drown
In the intricate sea
Of knowledge, memory, and challenge.

The Soccer Cup
by Antonio Fiocca

The boy was ready to play,
and he practiced a lot.
The game has started,
and he wasn't scared at all.
He knew what was going on,
and he knew how to score a goal.
So he got the ball,
and he dribbled to the net.
He dribbled like Messi,
and shot like Ronaldo.
And now he shot it,
and scored the winning goal!
The boy and his team,
have won the Soccer Cup!

Travel
by Mackenzie Kolar

Bright, not bright enough to be a cloud
A tinted cloud
A "peach cloud"
It's beautiful as it flows across the sky
A raindrop from the cloud
Down into the deep, ocean floor,
Many colors to discover
Light, but darker than light
A smooth creamy light
Almost like a coral,
A "coral cream"
A lovely color to look at
You almost want to blush
You blush as you look at it
Orange, not orange, but a lighter pink orange
It's very pure
Pure and specific
Like a bite of something sweet
An apricot
A ripe apricot
A "blushing apricot"
It sizzles in your mouth
Delicious

Spring A.K.A. Green
by Brianna Odgers

I turned and glanced out the window
the snow had melted leaving the ground green,
really green, lots and lots of green.
The green grass showed all over my backyard
it had come!!! Finally ... Spring.
I examined the trees, hard.
It seemed as if lady luck had knocked on my door
And all over the green grass lay a formal garden
Green, green, lots of Green, too much green.
it's as if I had fallen into a green trance.
All I imagined was green, everywhere
every spot, every crumble, every hole, green
Say good-bye to winter and say hello to spring,
A.k.a. Green

Simplicity
by Meghan Cook

Life would be easier if everything we did didn't matter
That if you made one mistake,
Not everything would fall apart
And you could stand small problems.
But life is in no way perfect
And although you try your hardest
Not everything goes right
And although you continue onward
Not everything is fine
But every now and then,
Everything does go right
Something perfect happens
And makes you love life
But this rare event
Does not outweigh all of the bad
It just makes it mildly more bearable
Not entirely worth it,
Just good enough that you'd be
Worse off without it

The Forest
by Anthony DiSandro

The tall trees
Cold, breezy winds
Animals running freely, not being harmed
The sun shining dimly on the ground
Peaceful, peaceful times
Then, "BAM!"
A tree falls down
Birds and squirrels run rapidly
Disoriented, they try to find a new home
People come through, building, chopping, and harming animals
The people leave.
The animals are happy again
Peaceful and free
The forest is calm again

The Animal Within Me
by Makayla Hess

There is a lone wolf inside me
With tattered teeth from fights never won
And like a Reaper's long blade
It has paws that trot as steady as a drum
The howling is its song of triumph, loneliness,
Hunger, and despair as it stalks through the midnight woods
As it howls it sounds like wind chimes
Being blown by warrior wind
It prowls its territory hungry for a fight,
But moves graceful and observant
The lone wolf lives inside my heart spiritually
And lives inside my head, dark, wise, and cunning
Like me.
It makes me feel like I can take my anger
And fear out on someone, but I can't
At least not yet ...
I wish it would live forever in my heart
The lone wolf is who and what I am.

Island Beach
by Cecilia Quirk

A speck in the sea of blue, a vacation getaway,
Its own little world away from stress filled days.
The blinding sun and its "candlelight yellow" rays
Wash all the other colors away.
My toes in the sand,
A refreshing glass of water in my hand.
The taste is complete with a "summer resort" colored citrus squeeze,
I gulp down the ice cold drink while I feel the cool breeze.
Farther inland, away from the shore,
Lies a great jungle with colors galore.
"Pear" colored leaves are part of the tropical fauna.
I rest under the colossal trees, grateful for their shade,
Because it is beginning to feel like a sauna.
The colors of this island, so bright and unique,
Make me wish I could stay for at least one more week.

The Boy On My Bus
by Christy Bilheimer

There was a boy who caught my bus every morning at 6:45
Whose eyes were as bluey-grey as the lake the kids go swimming in.
He'd sit with his friends and laugh at little things.
And when he wasn't laughing, he'd stare out the window watching the clouds.
I sit two seats behind him and I think he's beautiful.
There was a boy who caught my bus every morning at 6:45
Who lost the color in his eyes.
He still sat with his friends, but they never talked anymore.
I sit two seats behind him and I think he's beautiful.
There was a boy who caught my bus every morning at 6:45
Who was clinically depressed.
He'd wear long sleeves when it was hot out
And hide away from the teachers whenever he could.
I sit two seats behind him and I think he's beautiful.
There was a boy who committed suicide just a few days ago.
He wrote a letter to his parents saying that he was sorry about having to die.
He also wrote a letter to each of his friends telling them how much he loved them.
And one lonely letter sent to the girl who sat two seats behind him
Telling her that she was beautiful.

In the Attic
by Amelia Cusanno

You'll find me in the attic
Among swaying palm trees or in pine forests.
Sitting by a fireplace or on a sled sliding on a hill.
In the attic, I gather inspiration
And sketch it on paper.
Whatever I draw comes to life in my own little world.
In the attic, I am transported.
From someplace old and dusty like a temple
To somewhere new and fresh.
Don't ask me what I'm doing.
You will ruin the magic
Flowing out from my pencil.
In the attic, it is quiet
But I am never alone.
Nobody can find me in the attic.
Nobody except you.

Pond
by Alea Reilly

As the sun sinks lower into the darkening sky,
Its rays reflecting off the green water and bright sparkles of light
Lily pads at float with awaiting frogs croaking,
adding to the orchestra of Mother Nature's sounds
Specks of light fly around, filling the air with magic
Dragonflies racing in and out through the cattails that line the night sky
The weeping willow, like a huge dark shadow against the pale white moon,
letting its wispy leaves sink into the mass of darkness
Trickles of water as fish swim in the pond
The small breeze pushing the water over the pebbles that line the bank
The tall soft green grass sways in the wind,
As if dancing to the orchestra of nature
The moon tucks the gentle rolling land into a warm blanket
The air fills with the scent of lavender
As specks of purple dot the sea of green grass
All is quiet, yet the orchestra can be heard
All is still, yet alive with freedom and happiness
All is quite beautiful.

School
by Thomas Bennett

Lots of stress
And lots of work
Most kids got to it
Some do not
Assignments to finish
And essays to write
So much to do
In so little time
Some classes
You enjoy
Some you don't
And some are just boring
All of these things
Have something in common
And that is school

The Future Star
by Mario Venneri

The musician stole the show,
and told them not to leave.
It was the one and only Kenny G.
Playing all his glorious tunes.
It was an honor to meet him,
one day, I hope to be like him.
When I was young,
I hummed all his tunes.
When I played my saxophone,
I sit tall and relax.
When I got older, I improved greatly,
so I became one of the best.
With all my blues and jazz,
the crowd became to rejoice.
So I started to play two more instruments,
I had the talent to try them all.
I soon became the future star.

The Ocean's Force
by Micah Koss

I feel the frigid water around me,
I hear the crash of the ocean waves
A hand reaches down and pulls me up,
The sun's rays warm my body
I hear the crash of the ocean waves,
I feel the tug of the sea on my ankles
The sun's rays warm my body,
My legs go out from under me
I feel the tug of the sea on my ankles,
A wave crashes down above me, pushing me down
My legs go out from under me,
Gravity is keeping me down
A wave crashes above me, pushing me down
I feel the frigid water around me,
Gravity is keeping me down
A hand reaches down and pulls me up

The Boys From Massachusetts
by Deidre Deischer-Eddy

The boys from Massachusetts
They both wore ebony frames over their sapphire eyes
We were the three musketeers
I miss them when they're not around
They both wore ebony frames over their sapphire eyes
Sometimes I was the commander to their secret agent
I miss them when they're not around
I'll never forget them
Sometimes I was the commander to their secret agent
I think of our brief times together often
I'll never forget them
The older one saluted last time we said good-bye
I think of our brief times together often
We were the three musketeers
The older one saluted last time we said good-bye
The boys from Massachusetts.

Dreams
by Irini Ramizi

Dreams take you to a whole different dimension,
They give a chance to escape the real world.
And there is no doubt,
That's what I will be thinking all night about.

A Little Carefree Child
by Jordan Freud

My mother caught me off guard asking me to put away my jump rope,
    a pile of sidewalk chalk, and my imagination.
The command from my father was simple as ever,
    "Please take a seat and don't talk."
My brother asked if we were in trouble, while my other brother laughed saying,
    "Aren't we always?"
An emotionless look of solitude embraced my father's usual content face.
The command from my father was simple as ever,
    "Please take a seat and don't talk."
So I sat down in a wooden chair at my kitchen table,
    but an energetic little girl never stops talking.
An emotionless look of solitude embraced my father's usual content face.
The look on my mother's face was new, a combination or worry
    and that fake smile a mother always has to wear.
So I sat down in a wooden chair at my kitchen table,
    but an energetic little girl never stops talking.
My father spoke some foreign words, but I got the point– my mother was sick;
    my mother had cancer.
The look on my mother's face was new, a combination or worry
    and that fake smile a mother always has to wear.
I kept my little mouth shut because even a small kid knows
    that this cannot be good and I was worried I might lose my mom.
My father spoke some foreign words, but I got the point– my mother was sick;
    my mother had cancer.
My brother asked if we were in trouble, while my other brother laughed saying,
    "Aren't we always?"
I kept my little mouth shut because even a small kid knows
    that this cannot be good and I was worried I might lose my mom.
My mother caught me off guard asking me to put away my jump rope,
    a pile of sidewalk chalk, and my imagination.

My Sick Days
by Lais Santoro

Fumes of antibiotics and sickness wafted through the air
Blank walls, bruised body
Fingerprints all over from being held down
Unable to walk, talk or stand
Blank walls, bruised body
Medication running through my veins
Unable to walk, talk, or stand
But there will be hope
Medication running through my veins
Constantly tired and aching
But there will be hope
It's starting to light up within me
Constantly tired and aching
Fingerprints all over from being held down
It's starting to light up within me
Fumes of antibiotics and sickness wafted through the air

The Gateway
by Abirami Murugadoss

The boiling sun stings our skin as we walk by
We walk down the dirt path
I open the rusty green gate
Dragonflies pass by us as we try to catch them
We walk down the dirt pat
There lies a dirt road
Dragonflies pass by us as we try to catch them
We can see animals roaming the streets
There is a little creek filled with water
There lies a dirt road
I can see a small old temple
We can see animals roaming the streets
There is a little creek filled with water
I can see a small old temple
The boiling sun stings on our skin as we walk by
There is a little creek filled with water
I open the rusty green gate

Dolphin Girl
by Kennedy Riley

I walk shyly to the platform
Silence, a drip echoes in the distance
Cool, salt water ripples in a lifeless pool of wonder
Nothing, silence
A black speckled dolphin pops its slick head from beneath the surface
It swiftly slices through the water
Come with me! You'll be safe!
I swiftly jump into the water as in engulfs me
Welcome, to my home
Dolphins of the iciest blue and the most vibrant grey swirl around me
Stay with us, play in the embodiment of our dreams
Live in peaceful tranquility
And when night falls gaze at the stars
And remember us, Dolphin Girl
You are as radiant as the sun
Now go, dream a dream just like this one
Then I awoke

This Too Shall Pass
by Sami Uggla

I was told I have had it since my early years, the years of innocence.
I never realized what it was until much later on in my life.
Sometimes, I wish I could be someone else.
ADHD has taken over my life, turning it upside down.
I never realized what it was until much later on in my life.
It is like a demon is always controlling my mind.
ADHD has taken over my life, turning it upside down.
I disguise from the world, like a mask.
It is like a demon is always controlling my mind.
I feel like my life is at its toughest point.
I disguise it from the world, like a mask.
But I know that this too shall pass and the sunshine will come back.
I feel like my life is at its toughest point.
Sometimes I wish I could be someone else.
But I know that this too shall pass and the sunshine will come back.
I was told I have had it since my early years, the years of innocence.

Transformation
by Jessica Wright

The slush of my feet in the mud
The laughter of the cruel kids surrounding me
The words that shoot me like a gun
My muscles tighten as I try to avoid it
The laughter of the cruel kids surrounding me
I clamp my eyes shut
My muscles tighten as I try to avoid it
But it's too late
I clamp my eyes shut
I feel the pain of everything forming
But it's too late
I'm transforming already
I feel the pain of everything forming
The slush of my feet in the mud
I'm transforming already
The slush of my paws in the mud

Music
by Taylor Green

Your melodic rhythms and your profound lyrics soothe me
They sweep me off of my feet and help me drift away
As if I were lying in a boat in the middle of the ocean
You bring me a smile when I am sad, scared, and alone
You are a lamp for my feet and I let your light guide me
Through a path of prosperity when I am completely lost without hope
You lend me a hand when I am trapped in my own paradox
When I need something to relate to, you are the perfect companion
You've kept me from dying of complete boredom, you feed my soul
You've kept me from going insane, you've been my best friend
You've never broken a promise, you've never hurt me
With you time just seems infinite, you can entertain me for hours
But you haven't just helped me, you help others as well
You bring people together, you help them connect
You help people express themselves, you inspire many
You set imaginations ablaze like pouring propane on a burning fire
You help people release their creativity, the artist inside of them
You have saved people by helping them escape the bad in their minds
And you immediately took them on a faraway journey to the good
You are a savior, a guardian angel to most, you are music.

Orange
by Brandon McCoy

What is orange?
Warm in the sun and juicy as can be,
It's the color orange.
Orange is as warm as the sun.
Orange is a fresh, juicy fruit.
It is a piece of light in the warmth.
Orange makes a whistle in the light of the world.

My Choice
by Thomas Becker

Seats at lunch are always bad
So we are always sad
If only we could pick our seat
But now we have to plan a feat
And since you won't meet our demand
We will have to take a stand
Let us sit
Or we'll have a fit

The Burning Bush
by Grace Mailey

I sprinted atop the carpeted bushes,
Dangerously leaping across the gorge in the brush.
The knotted branches breaking the skin,
Missing the Cliff on the other side.
Dangerously leaping across the gorge in the brush,
I refrained from tearing.
Missing the Cliff on the other side,
The burn from the rug starting to sting.
I refrained from tearing,
Limping with leg now numb.
The burn from the rug starting to sting,
Not to dance that day no more.
Limping with leg now numb,
I sprinted atop the carpeted bushes.
Not to dance that day no more,
The knotted branches breaking the skin.

Winter
by Mya Howard

Everything is white
The cold breeze touches my face
Having fun outside

The Practice
by Shane Newell

As you get your helmet on
you feel the rush of adrenaline flow through you
You start your lap and at that moment
You know it's going to be a good season
You see the coaches talking
Then they call you over to talk and the moment
You know it's going to be a good season
As you start your drills
you sweat and have pains and at that moment
You know it's going to be a good season
At that end of the night you run like no tomorrow
At that moment
You know it's going to be a good season.

Abnormal
by Allyson Rea

Fear is rocks with algae growing all over them
As your feet touch them it's like a million needles shooting right up your spine
Slimy, slippery, fuzzy, hairy
Fear is like wandering through a haunted house
Struggling to walk through tons of slime
Fear is like scampering through graveyards
Filled with snapping turtles tightly packed together
Fear is a ghost haunting your heart,
Withdrawing your soul from your body into theirs
Fear is cliff diving off a five hundred foot tall cliff
Jump, fall, splash
Drifting closer and closer to the Earth's core
Never returning to the surface for air
Saying goodbye to everyone and everything around you

Snow Day
by Olivia McNeal

I sit, sit there in class, then
The sound came aloud on the overhead
Students, we will be having a half day today
The snow is getting high, it's about 3 to 4 inches.
We all stand and cheer aloud.
We all board the bus.
And now I sit, sit there on the bus.
We talk loud and we shout yay, yay, yay.
I can't wait as we arrive at my stop.
To jump into my nana's arms.
We walk home in the cold, cold snow.
Go inside and get in my snow gear.
I jump back out the door into the cold, cold. wet ...
S
N
O
W
I get up and say, "Let's go in now, please."
I get in and Nana makes me hot cocoa.
Then we sit, sit there and fall asleep.

The Hockey Tournament
by Kahlee Perera

Played all day, bodies sweaty
Losing daylight, but sticks still ready
Way in the back, I'm all alone
I take a deep breath, the whistle is blown
I watch the girls battle, and fight for the ball
It's hit around the field, just like a rag doll
Sticks clashed together, but we were now in control
Our team took it to the net, and we scored our first goal
We scored many more, the other team did, too
But our team worked together, and managed to pull through
The game finally ended, though I can't recall the score
We gathered around our coaches, tired and sore
We cheered and we cheered, and couldn't help but embrace
On that fateful day, our team won second place

Tick-Tock
by Alexandria Comly

Tick-Tock
Children share excited glances
Tick-Tock
Pencils roll off desk into school bags
Tick-Tock
The teacher smiles
Tick-Tock
With a ring, the children launch out the door
Tick-Tock
Hello summer

Green
by Sarah Lieberman

The fresh mowed grass
The leaves on trees
With the salad on my plate
To the monster on TV
The lucky color
The yucky color
From dark olive to a lime
With lizards and frogs covered in slime
A signal of keeping the environment clean
All of these things mean green.

My Tree
by Kendall Clarke

That's my tree in the front yard,
Standing there with the wind blowing hard.
In the fall its leaves fly with the wind so high,
Soaring like a bird through the sky.
That's my tree in the front yard,
Standing bold and strong.
The wind is the music outside,
And my tree is dancing along.
That's my tree in the front yard,
Smiling with glee.
Good thing I'm smiling too,
Because I'm happy that's my tree.

All My Fault
by Isabelle Marceau

Daddy, I'm so sorry
I didn't mean to make you cry
I can't tell you how it hurt
Seeing those tears slide out your eye
It's not your fault she hates me
That's just the choice she made
I wish we could just talk it out
So we both don't feel betrayed
She shut me out of many things
Her life and powder room
Sending my joy back inside me
To lay forever in its tomb
I try not to let it bother me
But cry in my sleep each night
I try my best not to get upset
But tears often cloud my sight
I'm crying as I write this
I hope that you can see
Daddy, you did nothing wrong
No, it was all only ever me

The Tire
by Shreya Mitra

It was a dark and rainy Sunday
Around the crazy yet peaceful highway
Almost all was silent until a loud thump was heard
Puzzled looks happened about
Around the crazy yet peaceful highway
A sharp and rocky turn was made
The car screeched and stopped at exit 13
Still, puzzled looks happened about
They stepped outside of the dented vehicle
As the hard rain poured down on them
They looked at the popped tire
Every second more they stood there, the darker it became
Still, the hard rain poured down on them
Still, they stood there with a popped tire
Still, it got darker every second more they stood there
Still, it was a dark and rain Sunday

My Cats
by Lillian Hecht

My cats are weird fuzz balls.
Tyler and River are drama queens,
And Izzie has paws like a human hand.
My cats may not be the most ordinary cats,
But they're mine.

Brothers
by Jacqueline Haitz

Why does he have to be older?
He so wishes he was bolder!
He loves to make my life miserable
He thinks he is irresistible
I guess I have to love him
But if I didn't, would that be a sin?
Why does HE have to be my brother
Dare to dream ...

Miki Doesn't Share
by Marissa Harley

One sunny Thursday afternoon,
I believe it was sometime in June,
Small, selfish Miki was at daycare,
And one thing she always did not do was share.
"No!" was always the answer,
Lisa asked for the pink crayon to color her dancer,
Miki didn't care if her dancer needed pink slippers,
Because her dolphin needed pink flippers!
She was as stubborn as a rock,
Her daycare instructors would try to get her to share with sweet talk.
Miki didn't share her seashells, not even the ones that were super sandy,
Her parents couldn't even get her to share her Halloween candy!
"No!" was always the answer, and always will be,
Miki had a problem that made everyone angry.
She never got a job, and the one time she did,
She wouldn't share her pencils and they called her a kid.
So life went on without any troubles,
Besides the fact Miki wouldn't even share her bubbles.
At the age of 50 she still couldn't share,
Despite the times they tried in daycare.

Swoosh
by Re'em Aviam

Swoosh goes the basketball
As it travels through the net
Like a car under a bridge
And flies through the air.

Manhunt
by Alex Haefner

The cool summer night,
The soft glow of the moon,
The night for manhunt.
I sprint through the dark
The tap of my shoes go pitter-patter pitter-patter
The soft rustle of leaves as I hop through the tree
Rough bark
Soft leaves
Silence
Darkness
The scent of flowers
The stress of the moment
He finds me
I run yet again through the night
This was my game of manhunt

Family
by Benjamin Wolfe

Family is like a house
there to shelter you
be with you
and stay with you all your life
some houses are small and some really big
and some not that strong
but what matters is your house is there
Family is a net
there to catch you when you fall
some nets soft warm cozy
some hard rough old scratchy
as long as they catch you.

Seasons
by Sara Hedglin

Summer
bright, beautiful
swimming, relaxing, playing
sun, water, Antarctica, ice
sledding, building, plowing
cold, white
winter

The Flower
by Sera Russo

As I look into the distance
I see a forgotten flower.
And as I breathe in its fumes
I feel drops of water on my skin,
And so does the flower.
The sound of whimpering is drawn to my attention,
And I glare at the flower,
I realize it is her.
So I shield her from the rain until the storm has passed.

Sky
by Adit Awatramani

High above in the blue, bright world
With the cold breeze tingling my skin
I can hear the wind swishing through my nose
Sky, sky, sky all the way up high.
When the time comes you turn orange
Then pink, dark blue and steadily pitch black,
Then once again you start to shine
During dawn I can't believe my eyes!
This cycle goes on 24/7
Dark and then bright like switching lights
The sun shines you in the morning
And the moon torches you in the night.
Sky, sky, you do so much for us
Our thanks can never pay you off
From bright to dark and dark to bright
Sky, sky, sky all the way up high.

That Little Boy Up There
by Alex Siaton

That little boy up there,
With birds and the trees
And flowers and bees
The long green grass
With a cool summer breeze
That little boy up there,
With the birds and the trees
That little boy up there.

My Dog
by Tara Shores

I came home from school,
Very bad news filled my brain.
My dog had just been put to sleep.
She was like a bright light
Every time she walked into the room.
My heart is an empty nest,
But she will always be my perfect dog,
Forever.
– To my former dog, Gidget

The Walk Along the Beach
by Dan Kelly

It was a calm, happy day
In the sunset
Walking with my mom and dad
On my birthday
In the sunset
Going on the hot sand
On my birthday
Near the vast blue ocean
Going on the hot sand
Along the beach
Near the vast ocean
Close to the end
Along the beach
Walking with my mom and dad
Close to the end
It was a calm, happy day.

Feeling Small
by Jonathan Frederick

When nobody is there to talk,
When you just want to scream,
People say to go on a walk,
That assumption is on the way you seem
Just let your heart open,
Don't feel small.
Although you feel broken,
Tell them all.
Let them know how you feel,
Stand up tall.
Don't sit back and squeal,
Don't be small.
Let your heart spray,
All the things you wanted them to hear.
What you always wanted to say,
Now they see you are here.
No matter what they say,
Let your heart out.
Frolic and play,
For when you try go all-out.

The Gunman
by Sana Gold

Hearing gunshots everywhere,
Smell of blood in the air.
People screaming,
Shooters scheming.
Looking around for somewhere to hide,
But soon you'll just be pushed aside.
Why must these people have their guns,
They pull them out and everybody runs.
Sometimes the catastrophe isn't this grand,
But why can't these guns just be banned.
If these issues went away,
All the kids could go out and play.
Dashing through a crowd as it parts,
With no fear of gunmen in their hearts.

Fun
by Aydin Buchanan

Friends and family
Oh how much fun they can be
we play together
I hope it lasts forever
and I hope it never ends

Soccer
by Samantha Neris

I put on my numbered shirt
Just like we rehearsed
I run on the green grass
Bees fly past
Sweat dripping from my head
Heart beating so fast I feel the dread
I stand my position, never switching
Ball is in my lane, I guess it's no pain, no game
Legs feel tore, I know after I'll be sore
But I shot my winning score.

Dreams
by Dejuan Russell

Lifting up out of my body
As I look at myself sound asleep
A white light reflects from the window
Catching my eye dramatically
My curiosity forces me to follow the light
I leave my body knowing I'm safe and sound asleep
I walk through the wall
Surprised that I can walk through the wall
To the outside world I've never seen before
Big steel gates await me as they open to
A neverland never seen before
Gravity leaves my feet with a tingle at the toes
As I begin to fly
Castle, towers, horses with wing
And with a blink of the eye
Mom is yelling at me
I'M LATE FOR SCHOOL!

Ice Cream
by Phoebe Vella

Pints, gallons, quarts
There are all sorts.
Chocolate, vanilla, strawberry,
You could even add a cherry.
Or if you want you can also try,
And have it with some pie.

My Home
by Aiden Perkins

My safe haven,
My palace,
My place I can be safe,
My home is all these things,
And I love it for all those things.

Spring
by Hayden Davis

Spring will be here soon
All the flowers will start to bloom
Petals all different colors;
Yellow, green, and even red.
Tiny seedlings in the mulch filled flower bed
Playing outside in the sun all day,
But first the snow needs to melt away!

Scars
by Molly Gray

The world is not a perfect place
Everyone lives
Everyone suffers
Everyone dies
The thing is
People tell you to do something with your life
Leave a mark on this world
But those marks are too often scars

My Day of Snow
by Dalton Whedbee

When I was sledding, all there was was snow.
All I wanted was to jump, but all I did was flump.
We wanted to get high, so we started to fly.
We were trying to ride, but all we did was slide.
So we tried to line it up, but then we messed it up.
Whenever we all go down, we managed to all fall down.
We were trying to fix this, but all we did was mix this.
So we all went in for the night, and we had a big fight.
We felt like going to bed 'til we heard what Cade said.

Magnificent May
by Samantha Cooper

May flutters in,
her dress covered in beautiful flowers,
her smile, as bright as a ray of sunshine,
brings warm weather and longer days,
May brings in Cinco de Mayo,
a day filled with sombreros and huge fiestas
Memorial Day marches in not far behind,
bringing American flags for all to enjoy,
Tiptoeing away, May says goodbye
as June quietly sneaks in
bringing green leaves instead of flowers
and even longer hours

The Wind Beneath My Wings
by Charlie Andress

It sweeps me off my feet
It keeps me going every day
Wondering what will happen next
Will they be there for me
Will they help me through my difficulties and hard times
Yes, Yes, Yes, Yes
They will always be there for me
Helping me every step until I feel I can touch the sky
The wind beneath my wings
My Family

Blue
by Andrew Iannacone

The color blue
reminds me of the ocean,
And the whirling of the wind,
I feel the summer breeze,
and the coolness of the pool.
I taste the cotton candy
melting in my mouth.
I smell the rainstorm petrichor
That makes me feel calm.

iPhone
by JunYoung Yoo

iPhone is my friend
My friend is an Apple.
Apple. Liked by magician
Magician has a wand
Wand goes bing bing
Zing zing
My friend, iPhone

Darkness
by Emily Fabian

The whole world was dark
Sad memories played on repeat
Tired of living in fear and loathing
Lying down feeling empty and lifeless
Sad memories played on repeat
Excruciating pain inside
Lying down, feeling empty and lifeless
All you feel anymore is hatred, disrespect, and emptiness
Excruciating pain inside
Hope everything will soon get better
All you feel anymore is hatred, disrespect, and emptiness
Keeping everything bottled up inside
Hoping everything will soon get better
Tired of living in fear and loathing
Keeping everything bottled up inside
The whole world was dark

Wind Beneath My Wings
by Ryan Spanier

The wind has taken me.
The birds are leading me.
My wings are flying me.
I drift through the air as my
hair is blown by the wind.
I am being pushed up higher
and higher from the
wind beneath my wings.

To Kick a Soccer Ball
by James Muldowney

When I was alone the day before,
I learned a new way on how to score.
In soccer there is a very hard way,
To kick the ball so it does not sway.
Its called the knuckle and it does not curve,
It does not spiral, spin, snake, or swerve.
To do this, you must kick with power,
It will take years of practice (or maybe one hour).
When you get it right and the ball goes in the goal,
A wave of happiness will crash on your soul.
But don't learn it from me, I only did it once,
And the other times I tried, I looked like a dunce.

I Don't Know
by Merrit Wenhold

I don't know what to write.
Maybe I'll grab a bite
let's avoid the fight
and agree I cannot write
I'll write about an orange
wait the only thing that rhymes with orange is door-hinge
unless you make a word up like boringe
or like noringe, korhinge, bloringe, and grohinge
I almost finished but I don't know what to do
three more lines till you boo
this will all turn to goo
go ahead and boo!

The Killing Tide
by Louis DeLuna

A stillness at first
Whirlpools and currents move in
Rip you out to sea

The Woods
by Mark Gundrum

Being in my woods
Makes me feel good
I like to walk my dog
Right by the big logs
I like to climb
Up in the pines
Watching all the deer
Eat up the ears
Watching the hawks fly
Right by my tall trees
The wind passes with ease
Right by me
Oh what a beautiful sight to see

The Race To Freedom
by Ella Spencer

It's like a race–
Without ribbons and prizes.
We keep running, no matter what,
And don't stop until we win.
This is the gay rights movement.
We came from the 1960s,
When homosexuals couldn't appear in public
Without risk of being arrested.
And we keep on running.
Because soon,
Massachusetts legalizes gay marriage,
Other states to follow.
The race becomes more intense.
But every day, more say yes
And we are winning
And hopefully soon,
We will cross the finish line.

Believe
by Divya Pillai

No one will try to hear my voice,
That is their choice
We're as lonely as we let it be.
It's true so why don't you believe?
There's many people passing my way,
They never hear what I have to say
No one is there to stand by my side.
Maybe that's because everyone has something to hide.
Why can't they at least acknowledge me?
Your decision is the key.
I say the truth,
They say I'm caught up in my youth
I'm wiser than you may think.
Even if you ignore me I won't shrink.
Life is easier if you dare to care.

Just Because I'm Girly
by Jackie Wynman

Just because I'm girly ...
Don't think I dress nicely
Don't think I walk instead of run
Don't think I can't be tough because I can
I am tough, I can be a gorilla.
Just because I'm girly ...
I don't text on my iPhone all day
I don't watch Mean Girls
I don't wear pink every day
I don't flip my hair all the time
Just because I'm girly ...
Doesn't mean I can't like black
Doesn't mean I wear a lot of make up
Doesn't mean I like wearing yoga pants
Doesn't mean I hate getting wet
Just because I'm girly ...
I wouldn't like other colors like purple and white
I wouldn't cry over something so little
I wouldn't like sports but I do
Just because I'm girly– please treat me differently

Window
by Rachel Tercha

Windows give you a slight taste of the world around you.
All of the brutal weather is not coming in and I'm not going out.
Some window views are beautiful, nice, and bright,
While others are forlorn, dark, and dull.
Sometimes it's not even worth cleaning your window, sometimes it would be
Better just to crawl back into bed and cuddle under your blankets.
But occasionally, it's nice to wake up and take a quick peek
At what's coming up next.

Fun Is Everything
by Briana St John

As the wind zipped around the sky
The willow tree makes laughter high
The long thick branches of leaves hanging with loads of fun
Being weighted down from kids
With happy hearts singing and galloping
They play till the sun is at its peak
The kids left with a joyful seek
Fun is everything but it's all gone
Now that the kids have left for a run
The tree in the sun will weep till it's done!

Broken
by Madison Snyder

You thought that I was okay,
That everything was just fun and games,
But what you don't know is that I hide behind a fake smile,
It's like walking on fire and broken bottles.
The person you see in front of you,
She isn't real, she isn't true.
The pain runs fluently through my veins,
Along with all my motionless shame.
You don't understand this is all for you,
I only want our friendship to be true,
But I cannot do that if I fake this smile,
I cannot do it unless I stop all my sorrows.
I just hope you understand,
I just want to be your friend until the end.

Becoming Winter
by Cloe DiFlumeri

A blanket of white cloaks the ground under my feet.
A gray sky floats far above me,
Peppered with small twinkling snowflakes.
The soft coo of mourning doves ripples into this world,
Sinking into the snow and landing in the tree branches.
Everything is moving in a slow and steady rhythm,
Like a song being played for the entirety of the world to hear.
This moment is its own world of silent music,
The smallest cog of the machine that is life and the living,
A piece of a puzzle;
The puzzle made up of the most beautiful moments in the history of this world.
It is here that I meet winter. The cold snow hugs me in sympathy.
The cold ground carpeting my fall.
As the cold wraps me in its loving grasp,
I close my eyes. I give in to the sweet melody.
I let it overtake me;
Become me. I give in. I let it take over.
I am drifting, drifting away.
I am ethereal.
I am fall.

The Future Being Told
by Casey Cannella

Through the hallways, feeling lonely
Into an immense school feeling smaller by the minute
I am full of mindful information
Feeling good through my first class
Feeling like I belong in the school
But, life goes on past high school
I must decide where to go
To choose between college or work
I list all the pros and cons
The place I belong is college
As I try to conceal my tears
Here I go, propelled into the big world
Going to college to face my fears and my future to come
The feelings I have for college are indescribable
College is where I want to be
Where I go to follow my dreams.

Baseball Season
by Matt Witkowski

April showers might bring May flowers,
But April brings baseball season.
Baseball season is Christmas for fans everywhere.
Fantastic, fanatic fans fill the stands for a promising season.
Teams fail to disappoint while appointing success.

Overrated
by Fiona Sweeney

At some point people find the flaws
This night just wasn't meant at all
Like a toy for child's play
Plastic molded end of day
At some point people say I'm wrong
For singing my depressing song
If watching, it was not my tool
At midnight I'd remain a fool
And here I sit, sublimely still
As my thoughts run wild and shrill
My lonely vigil with the moon
Whilst others run into their tombs.

Every Step
by Erika Kondo

The footstep from Japan
has taken root in the moist earth
and is already growing into a sturdy tree
with emerald leaves that gleam
like me but I'm more average height
with caramel skin
and a sly amethyst color heart
Prancing on the rocks in the river
I am like a lion cub
struggling every step of the way
and gathering courage to roar like a king should
I have big dreams but always hesitate to take action
that's how I walk right now
and it might be how I walk in the future

8:00 At Night
by Luke Percy

The winds are howling
But the comforter is warm
So I go to sleep

Soccer
by Max Hafer

As the ref blows the whistle,
The wind blows in my face,
The ball at my feet,
I begin to pick up my pace,
Beating every defender I see,
There is nowhere I would rather be,
I see the goalie out of his box,
I decide to take a shot,
All time seems to stop,
As the ball glides through the air,
When the ball smashes into the net,
The crowd goes crazy,
I know I have won the game.

Consumed
by Sean Polisano

Death, like quicksand, waiting for a stumble or slight slip.
And once you're stuck in this quicksand, you shall be stuck,
never being able to escape. Death, like an ocean that seems endless,
only death is endless, and it goes on forever holding you hostage.
You can search for a light, but you know that once death has consumed you
in darkness, you can't ever escape that darkness.
Death is a snake that keeps shaking its tail as a warning and reminder that it
can strike whenever it wants. Reminding us that it's in charge and we never
forget it. Like an endless ocean, death goes on forever. Like quicksand and
darkness consuming and holding you forever.
Only you can turn on a light to make the darkness go away, you can get rid of
the snakes, and you can dry and pollute the ocean.
But there's no getting rid of death, it will be around forever. And once we are
captured and devoured by death, it shall keep us there forever.
Death is an everlasting flame of life that will never burn out, until all humans
are dead. Because only then when all of us humans are forever gone will death
rule the planet we call Earth.

Her
by Kylie McNamee

Her
That horrible girl
Who I despise
Her wrath, never ending
Her ignorance, unstoppable
Her words like gunshots,
And her hand is on the trigger
One day best friends,
The next worst enemies.
Girls that made it through
Said it'll be alright
But that was hard to believe
She's tried to make me jealous
But I don't care
Since I've shed that extra layer of skin,
My new armor shines
I'm a warrior now.
She's taught me a lot,
About what not to be
So thank you, you horrible girl

Standing On Top of the Beam ...
by Mareena Scalia

Standing on top of the beam
Just waiting to go
Bursting with angst
I get voices in my head of disappointment in my head
Thinking about it just makes me want to jump off
But I can't
I can't because I need to do it
I need to persevere
Through the pressure and go
And when I do it
Everyone will be proud of me
But I'm still on top of the beam
Just waiting to go
Everyone is eyeing me up like
I'm the cheese and they are the mice
But the pressure is too immense
But I'm still on the beam
Just waiting to go

Bullies
by John Wodnick

The constant cruelty
The constant hate
I don't know them and they don't know me,
so I ask myself, why, why, why they keep trying
I feel like they think I'm trash
Just something they are happy to get rid of.
They say I'm a nerd or that I'm a bookworm
I always say, "You know what, nerds run the world."
And then just walk away

Here Comes the Bride
by Kayla Gillen

Here comes the bride,
Here comes the bride,
Feeling like a princess and walking like a queen.
Walking down the aisle in her beautiful white dress,
Feeling her heart pounding and taking those final steps.
Here comes the bride,
Here comes the bride,
Coming down the aisle, who is now a wife.

To This Day
by Cassie Force

To this day, I hate being called names
I am not the only kid who grew up this way
Surrounded by people who used to say rhymes
About sticks and stones as if broken bones
Hurt more than the names, we got called them all
So I grew up believing no one would ever fall in love with me
But then it got worse, I got called ugly, fat, and a lot of other stuff
But it wasn't far
Someone told me to look in the mirror
I did and I saw that those people who said that to me lied
I am not ugly, nor fat
I am pretty, I am not fat, but not skinny
I still get picked on every day, but I know that my life will get better
I believe in me

Hockey
by Mason Kay

You need to be bold
To go out on the ice, it's pretty cold
When you get hit
It feels like you've been bit
When you score a goal
You feel like a troll
The other team gets mad
But you don't feel bad
The other team wants to fight
And they'll fight with all their might

Tuscany
by Lauren Dachowski

Grass greener than you can imagine
Patchwork patterns of olive groves and grapevines
Ancient farmhouses barely standing
Rolling hills for miles and miles
Medieval cities with cobblestone roads
Wild boar salami and pecorino cheese shops
Wineries at every turn
Shops with leather goods for every taste
Scenic views that are like none other

School
by Tommy Mathewson

Name calling
Bullying
Stress
It's school
Homework
Working all night
Depression
It's school
Through tough times
School can be a metal detector
Tough to get through sometimes
But it's just school

Camping Season
by Emma Carbone

When there is no more cold white snow on the ground
You know it's spring
When you pack up your tent or camper you go, go, go
Then you open it up to unpack
It feels like opening up a Christmas gift
You sometimes get the joy of having your cousins there with you
At the playground, basketball and soccer as far as the eye can see
Racing from site to site
Stargazing on a fuzzy blanket
At the end of the night you gather around the campfire
Telling scary stories
Catching up with family members you missed
Roasting marshmallows to get that golden brown color
Then turning it in for the night, you know you're leaving then
You just want to make it last
The beautiful sight of nature
Kids nowadays need to see the world
Even if that means simply going outside

Halloween Night
by Julia Zambo

It was the night of Halloween
The sounds of soft footsteps and obnoxiously loud screams
Trick-or-treating starts at eight o'clock
All the children running while parents desire to walk
Skeletons in yards wrapped up in chains
And mortifying faces glaring through windowpanes
The leaves rustled and bustled through the crowded streets
And the sidewalks were walked on by tiny feet
The costumes ranged from aesthetic to grotesque
And decorations outside, didn't fail to impress
Owners of the houses told the children they looked dandy
As children begged people for more and more candy
Even though it's cold, children begin to sweat
And because kids sprint through yards, owners grow to be upset
Children stuff their mouths with sugary sweets
And scrutinize the roads for extra treats
When house owners run out of delicious snacks
And children can't see anything but pitch black
Eerie silence on the streets will come down
And besides the creaky street lamp there will be no sound

Crisp Paper
by Angeline Ma

Ivory sheets rustle
In the darkness of the library.
One girl devours a book
In a shady corner
As the staff whisper,
"We'll be closing soon."
Momentarily startled,
She glances up,
Only to return to the safety
Of the words that crawl on
The pages like
Ants over cream.

The Musician's Violin
by Samara St. John

With the graceful bow gliding across the strings
so calmingly he plays a tune.
He plays one last time before he presents his talent to the crowd.
He gathers his sheets, puts on a tie and
heads for the performance hall.
With one, two, three steps he makes his way on stage
with rumbling joy from the crowd.
Bowing once he begins to play.
Those once calming strings bellowing out
one of Beethoven's best pieces become strong and draw the crowd
into hearing a story only music can play.

Angels
by Alexa Artmont

When we're little, our parents tell us there are angels watching over us.
Winter, spring, fall, and summer angels.
They protect us from bad things in the world.
But, sometimes we wonder why we can't see them.
We know they're there. They tell us seeing isn't believing.
Believing is seeing. Just because we can't see them doesn't mean we can't believe.
Angels are everywhere in the world. When we're hurt they comfort us.
They make sure we we're alright. If we're feeling lonely or alone.
They're always there, and we know we're not alone.

Hippo
by Margaux Lestage

My stuffed animal hippo
Is my favorite animal
Soft and cuddly
When I hold it in my arms,
I know everything is going to be okay
Skinny, cute, and loving

My Heart, Your Eyes
by Chloe Rich

My heart stops,
When I look into your eyes.
My body freezes,
I become paralyzed.
All around me,
Nothing moves.
The sky turns a deep shade of blue.
All this happens when I look at you.

The Beach
by Greta Barnes

I walked across a plank, and onto the shore.
I sank my feet into the lush sand.
Feeling it squish against my toes.
The beach is silent.
I look up, seeing the beauty and splendor of it all.
The breeze gently blowing across my face,
Smelling of salt water and sand.
Waves calmly crashing onto the shore.
Folding at the last second, revealing their white foam.
It looks like a painting, with different strokes of color.
The orange, the pink, the yellow,
All brushed together and swirled around.
They say the beach is a quiet place,
I say that it is my place.
The beach is a masterpiece.

Live Your Life
by Rachel Kostival

We have a normal routine,
We get up, eat, and go,
This everyone does except some,
Some live life to the fullest,
Living life to the fullest is making a difference,
Making a change in our world,
Maybe for some it's exploring and learning,
And maybe it's soaking it all in,
The trees, the flowers, the fresh dew on the grass,
The rays of the sun, the puffs of clouds,
Take it all in,
Every day could be new and different,
Every day could be exciting,
Laughter, cheer, joy could be experienced,
All by living life to its fullest,
The sky's the limit,
So go see the world,
Meet new people, taste new things,
And live your life to its fullest,
For your life is a gift from God.

A Moment To Remember
by Hannah Peterson

My skis click into the bindings.
My stomach starts to turn.
I can hear a crunch under my worn boots,
As I glide into the start corral.
I hear a man count me down. 3, 2, 1!
I fly out into the trail.
My poles dragging everyone's eyes towards me.
I dodge every gate on my way down,
Slapping them with every turn.
I can taste the crisp air in my face.
The finish is up ahead,
My goal racing towards me
And off I go. Turn, slap, turn, slap.
And I've done it.
Cheers surround me and I am engulfed.
The winter has burnt my cheeks red,
But I stand in pride.
I win.

What Homework Does
by Jerry Ascolese

Homework gives me so much stress, so much stress it makes me depressed,
Homework makes me want to cry, I feel like I could just die.
So much work every night, I don't ever feel all right,
I get so tired and out of sorts, it makes my throat so very hoarse.
Then I finally go to sleep, I'm so exhausted I don't count sheep,
My alarm goes off I hit the snooze, I go downstairs and I'm confused.
I try to eat the food in front of me, but I'm so tired I can barely see,
I go back up and jump in the shower, my mom says not to take an hour.
But I'm so tired I fall in a trance, I get out and I take a glance,
The clock says that it's 6:30, and I've got to hurry.
I run and run straight down the stairs, like I'm being chased by bears,
I run straight into the garage, I feel as if I'm in a montage.
My mom drives the car so fast, she drives so fast I can feel the blast,
We're going so fast we hit warp speed, we're going so fast I almost peed.
She slams the brakes so darn hard, that my eyes get all starred,
We made the bus by the skin of our teeth, I walk on like I am elite.

The Key To Happiness
by Alana Bonilla

Struggle is the key to happiness,
It's not money nor sin,
No, that's fraudulent happiness,
In order to be happy,
You must first work hard,
You must endeavor through every obstacle that comes your way,
These are the true steps to happiness,
Without them you would never feel exhilaration
You can only feel happiness when you've felt defeat,
Then you will never want to feel it again,
You must fight through every battle like the world depended on it,
If you complete these steps you are guaranteed to feel joy,
You must know kindness like it was the back of your hand,
You must feel empathy for anyone that crosses your path,
You must struggle,
That's the key to happiness

Trouble
by Steven Hobaugh

The reason why I get in trouble
Is because I mess around with people
And throw stuff at them.
I try to control what I do
But I have trouble.
My mind moves like a rapid river.
Before I can control my movements
I am doing something I know that I should not do.
I do it for attention.
I do it for happiness at first.
Then I'm not happy.
I do it to make my mind happy.

Just Because ... I'm a Girl
by Kayla Nadot

Just because I'm a girl,
Don't think I'll wear skirts to school,
Don't think I'll have a ribbon in my hair,
Don't think I'll curl my hair every day,
Just because I'm a girl
Don't expect me to sign up for dance class,
Don't expect to be #1 cheerleader,
Don't expect me to spend every waking hour at the mall,
Don't expect me to have pillow fights every Fridays with my BFFs,
Just because I'm a girl,
Don't think I don't know the concept of football,
Don't think I won't know what a lay up is,
Don't think I won't know the difference between and goal and a touchdown,
Don't think I won't know who the Eagles are.
Just because I'm a girl,
Don't expect me to fantasize over boy bands,
Don't expect me to have my room painted pink,
Don't expect me to care if a boy likes me,
Don't expect me to not get an A in my classes.
Because trust me, I won't wear skirts, I understand sports,
I don't do dance and I don't like pink.

The End of Time
by Kelly Rothenberg

Cracking, rumbling ground
Violent waves overcome Earth
No more life is found

Thought
by Alex Lozada

Sometimes I sit and wonder,
about the things that I've done,
things I did long ago
or something that's only just begun.
Whether good or bad,
maybe a truth or a lie
I know I'll find an answer
sometime before I die.
My mind, an endless abyss,
seems to never end,
but sometimes I feel constantly
I out-think myself time and time again,
But if I don't figure them out
and it is all for naught
I hope someone does,
so that I didn't waste my thought.

Roller Coaster
by Marin Young

You stand alone no matter where you go
Standing out as much as white chocolate in a batch of dark chocolate
Your life is a roller coaster that you are forced to ride
And so far you have hated every minute
All alone on the roller coaster of life
But coming up behind you is another car on your roller coaster
Miraculously your cars connect
They have never separated since
Your roller coaster ride isn't as scary anymore
And never will be again

Marconi Macaroni
by William Marconi

I am a Sicilian donkey,
A sweet, affectionate, social creature,
At five foot three inches,
I fly gently through life like an orange kite,
I am a hard worker like the ant,
Big and bold, I am a rock,
I bounce through my days,
Being still isn't my way.

Celebrity Love
by Nicholas Bowman

I want to point out something I see:
Why is it that we look up to celebrities like kings and queens?
I shiver when I see them get away with non-legals,
And put up on pedestals like crosses on steeples.
I hate the thought of people thinking they're better
because they wear expensive shoes or a cardigan sweater.
I am not cringing nor am I crying,
and no, on the inside I am not dying.
I just make a plea to you on this one simple thing.
Don't treat celebrities better because they can sing.
Or because they can dance or because they can joke
or because they're sponsored by companies like Pepsi or Coke.
We give them all of our perfect attention.
But I am hissed at if I even question.
Please don't get me wrong, not all are bad.
Some are quite normal like your mom or your dad.
Some live simple, normal lives,
giving all their attention to their kids and wives.
But what about those who don't care for their fans,
leaving them in the cold and driving off in their vans?
They call a big meeting if they get a tan,
and think they are godly, like Jesus the man.
I want to point out something I see:
Sometimes I feel celebrities are unneeded like a spleen.
I am here to express myself and ask a simple question.
Am I a celebrity because you gave me all of your attention?

Mother's and Father's Day
by Jonathan Felter

Father's Day and Mother's Day are only a month apart
To celebrate our parents who play a big part.
From birth to lovely end,
They will love us even still.
Mothers are meant for hugs,
While fathers are meant for tugs.
When you're hurt they'll help you.
When you fall down they lift you up.
When these holidays roll around,
There's a joy that does abound.
I guess it's what I feel for you each and every day.
To celebrate the day, we look forward to surprises that lie at every bend.
I want you to know, that through everything,
I still love you

I Believe
by Patrick McIntyre

I believe spirituality is healthy and can do great things for you
I believe it can inspire you to be a better person
and is sharper than the strongest blade
I believe spirituality can be overdone and become an unhealthy reliant
I believe spirituality is not merely religion, but rather a gift
I strongly believe someone or something will always bring you up,
even if it's not sky high
I believe there is still hope in this lonely world
I believe we should not lose faith, for when misfortune surfaces
there is always a pinch of good
I believe the world is rich with opportunities and you just need to pursue them
I believe you have a place in the universe and the position you occupy is unique
I strongly believe someone or something will always bring you up,
even if it's not sky high
I believe you have to make your mark in life to be remembered
I believe life is a chance and you have to seize the possibilities around you
I believe life works in strange ways in unity with the universe
I believe life is worth more than any measure of riches,
and you don't know when it may reach its final page
I strongly believe someone or something will always bring you up,
even if it's not sky high

Where Am I?
by Christian Guthrie

Where am I?
What happened?
I have so many questions,
and only darkness to answer,
yet I feel more free than ever.
Here he can't reach me,
in this dark room.
This isn't so bad,
I may be slowly losing my sanity,
but at least it is quiet.
My eyes are starting to adjust to the dark,
and so is my heart.
That's not so bad though ...

Sam's Monkey
by Anna Needle

There once was a boy named Sam
And, yes, he had a monkey named Ham.
Now you are probably wondering why he had a monkey
The story is a little funky.
It all started at a zoo
Sam was screaming "boo whoo".
He was upset because he dropped his ice cream
So the monkey climbed over the beam.
He hopped on Sam's back
And gave him a little smack.
And that's where it all began.
Now Sam was a little guy
But he had a well behaved monkey by his side.
And this monkey was brave
There was action he craved.
So he jumped on a plane
And was caught by a chain.
He met up with Sam
Where Sam said, "S'up," to Ham.
By the way, they do something wacky every day.

The Color Yellow
by Hannah Simerson

There once was a girl with a goat
She kept it hidden in a boat
She let it run free
For it had to pee
And now she has a yellow coat

Changes
by Sadie Bushway

There are changes each day
Buds are popping, sap is done
The snow is melting away
The grass is greening up again
All the birds have come a long way
Back roads are muddy and ruddy
The sky is no longer gray
Spring has finally sprung!

Rather
by Sydney Badman

I would rather have the wind whisper in my ear,
Than have people whisper to me about rumors.
I would rather watch the waves crash,
Than see the gossiping snakes around me.
I would rather feel the green grass,
Instead of feeling fine expensive silk.
I would rather smell the flowers,
Than get the perfume that tries to duplicate it.
I would rather listen to words sung,
Instead of hearing them be spoken.
I would rather wake up thinking about how I can make a difference,
Instead of being concerned about my clothes and hair.
I would rather stand out in a crowd,
Than jumping on the bandwagon.
I would rather be me,
Than wearing the mask that throws my originality away.
I would rather know that I am the person I want to be,
Instead of feeling like I wasted a day, a day where I could have changed
and been the person that would make me happy and proud to be me.

Gone Fishing
by Jacob DeTreux

Fishing is my favorite pastime.
I love all the water and grime.
It teaches me to be patient and wait.
Oh crap! We've ran out of bait.

Kobe Bryant
by Aaron Joseph

Kobe Bryant, a 5 time NBA champion
He's also an Olympian
He was born in Philly
And he makes defenders look silly
When Kobe plays
He always shows great display
One game, Kobe scored 81
And that game had stunned everyone
And what makes Kobe truly amazing
When he's versus his opponents, he is always blazing

The Slow Motion Goal
by Erin Hooper

I dribble
I kick
I shoot and wait
The goalie stretches to catch her fate
I fling the ball straight at the goal
Power and strength upon my soul
I wish and hope for this one chance
The goalie thinks opposite taking a glance
I look to see everyone stop
The ball floating like a flying top
The crowd jumping in slow motion
To see if I did something atrocious
I feel reality coming back
It slaps me hard with a WHACK
People patting me on the back
My arms lift
My smile does too
We won the game
Something I never thought we'd do!

When Winter Ends
by Emma Flinchbaugh

If winter is over,
Where is the grass?
If winter is over,
Where is the sun?
It should be springtime,
But I might be wrong,
It probably still is winter.
Maybe snowmen are meant to be built,
Maybe snowballs are meant to be thrown.
It could fall,
I must be wrong!
Or maybe I'm dreaming,
So that means it must be summer.

Perseverant Me
by Meghan Hartey

Dark skies cover the world above, and it scares the birds and the trees.
But still I walk along.
The water runs in fear of the world, and there's no one in sight.
But still I walk along.
Wind screams and howls in my ear, and the rain stings my face.
But still I walk along.
Vultures pester from above, swarming my head, and my hands tremble.
But still I walk along.
But then I peer ahead and through the trees I see;
a hint of sun, a hint of day, a hint of hope.
I walk along.
What's behind me is in the past, and I won't ever look back at those buried terrors.
I walk along.
I will succeed, I will come out victorious, I'll never go back, and I'll never quit.
I walk along.
The sunlight is my motivation, it will embrace me tightly
and wash over me with its warm arms.
I walk along.
Triumph will rise inside me once I know I have made it
through this impossible battlefield.
I'll always walk along.

The Story of Jill
by Steven Yannett

There once was a boy named Phil
Who was friends with a girl named Jill.
Then one day
Phil ran away,
And Jack came to play with Jill.

A Broken Ankle
by Caroline Adams

Ah! Pop, snap, crack, split
Sacred Heart Gym and that one Elite sock
Scary, sad, shocked, confused
A blurred moment
Like I don't know where I am
As if you are alone and gone
A pulsing feeling
The brain begging for it to stop
It's official, broken
People staring
Stop!
Why can't it heal faster?
A broken ankle

Love
by Mackenzie Geroni

When I walk into the room
It is me and it is you.
I take your hand, pull you close.
I look into your shining eyes.
I see your soul and soon realize I will always love you.
Don't let me fall, but if I do will you catch me or will I catch you.
Don't let me go, pull me in and love me so.
If I love you will you love me too?
I have waited for this moment.
Hand in hand, you close to me, me close to you.
I have always loved you.

Snowflake
by Grace Korcheck

I can be big
Or I can be small
I have my own unique shape
Nobody else is like me
Nobody else looks like me
Not even my family
I have friends
Some highlight me
Some make me blend in
No matter what I look like
I am me

A Day That Drags On Forever
by Maria Fennell

The hands of the clock are glaciers
Taking eons to move
Words morph into hums
Slippery smooth sandy
Ragged and rough
Tired and gray
Tick
Tock
Tick
Tock
Tick
Tock
My lunch churns in my stomach
It is a shark
Why does time slow down?
How does time slow down?
Tired and gray
This day is dragging on forever
Tick
Tock
Tick
Tock
Tick
Tock

Summary Flow
by Nicolete Colón

Lets go to the beach
The ice cream truck is here now
Lights dance in the sky

A Colorful Gaze
by Austin Filippone

I see the bright yellow sun,
dropping a blanket of light on the earth.
I feel calm, staring out of the window in my living room.
I see the shed sitting calmly, wooden and dry.
To my left, I see a forest so calm and subtle.
Far away, I can see more houses and streets,
swallowed by tons of cars and people.
I wish I could take in this beauty forever.
A terrific, beautiful, colorful gaze.

Cheering Is a Sport
by Samantha Crum

It's about,
the team
the stunts
the coaches
and the tumbles.
Cheering is a sport,
for those who disagree,
we practice
we run
we jump
we compete
we exercise,
and we lift
not weights,
people.
Next time someone says
"cheering isn't a sport"
correct them because
it is a spot.

Grass
by Shannon Baker

Blowing in the wind
An endless sea of green
Deer ticks make their home

The Night
by Rebekah Hall

The night is for the people who run
without the fear of getting lost
They were running through the woods
leaving no path behind
They reached upon a nearby cabin with the look of hope.
The cabin was small and worn down,
but the boy and girl saw hope in its repair;
just like their paths
For they did not know that this cabin
would be the start of a new beginning.

Seasons
by Joyce Dowd

Spring
Still blooms
with colorful flowers and beautiful plants
From the cold bright white winter
As it did last year
Winter
is still cold
with kids playing in the snow
and people shoveling the sidewalks
as it did last year
Summer
is hot as people swim
in the swimming pool and in the ocean
as it did last year
Fall
brings color in the trees and ground as winter begins
we all get ready for the cold winter ahead
as it did last year

Dogs vs. Cats
by Kaylee Rodriguez

Puppies
silly, smart
nibbling, running, playing
park, shelter, mouse, string
hissing, jumping, fighting
evil, quiet
kittens

Thousands of Miles Away
by Emily Flora

Thousands of mile away
Lived a girl,
Who loved a boy,
With every breath she took.
The boy did not love her,
That was certain.
The girl was told
It wasn't right to have such feelings
For a boy who
Could not return them.
Yet, thousands of miles away;
When the boy smiled,
The girl smiled too,
Knowing it was worth it.

Overcome It
by Riley McDade

The thing that holds you back can't keep you forever,
The thing you let rule your life won't last.
Take that thing that overpowers you in your palms,
And crush them in your fists,
You can go whatever your imagination takes you.
Let your good memories flow throughout your soul,
And all your good times mold you into believing.
Once you're done, you should feel three things,
You should feel alive!
Feel like even the biggest boulder can't crush you!
Especially, feel INVINCIBLE!
Overcome it.

Man With a Large Nose
by Carter Maberry

There once was a man with a large nose
Who dreamed of doing a pose
One so great
It will fill his enemies with hate
But I think it will not happen, I suppose

Moonlight
by Katherine Konstantinidis

The moon shines bright
in the cool summer night
then a few stars
aligned with Mars
it is beautiful tonight

My Hero, Batman
by Peter Butterline

Batman might not fly
but he can still fight bad guys
He is a hero

Glistening Snow
by Katie McIlvaine

The children play,
The angels sway,
And the snow is
Beautifully glistening.
An still one day,
The snow will slowly,
Slowly melt away.
The trees, so bright,
And when it's night,
They glisten by the moon.
What the weatherman said,
I'm sure is right,
But I am still in bed.

Springtime
by Jenna Burns

A flower's a magnificent thing
Some may say it mimics the sound of spring
Vivid colors blooming
The world's moving
Now it's almost time for the bell to ring

Trouble
by Danielle Arters

I'm suspended,
Now I'm happy.
I'm kicked off the bus,
Now I'm free.
Back talking to people,
I don't want to be quiet.
It's another fight,
Another detention.
I don't care if people notice.
Not willing to change,
Wanting to be diverse.
Strolling through the halls,
Thinking about yelling.
It's the end of the day,
I'm out of control.

Nature At Night
by Sierra Stukes

The shining light glistens as
Bright as a star
I watched it from afar
The lilies bloom
In the light of the moon
Others only at noon
When the sun goes down
And everything's silent
All of the plants
Will be very quiet

Who I Am
by Danielle Otery

I'm a hero who saves the world
I'm a performer whose acting is brilliant
I'm an athlete who pushes her limits
I'm a singer who has the voice of an angel
I'm a writer who writes out her thoughts
I'm a dancer who keeps believing
I'm a musician who follows her dreams
I'm a fighter who fights for freedom
I'm a gamer who never gives up
I'm a wizard who fights evil
I'm a student who works hard
I'm a cheerleader who cheers for the Pirates
I'm a lover who loves her life
I'm a miracle who was sent by God
I'm a friend who will help you out
I'm a cousin who is the best one ever
I'm a Ukrainian who is also American
I'm a girl who lives two separate lives
I'm an Otery who is amazingly amazing

Orange Baseball
by Matt Petrillo

A soft bouncy crust
Orange
Put on leather and laces
Stood above the sand
Weeds everywhere
The bases aren't put in
No cleat marks
No bats, gloves, and helmets
Just fences
The best part of the year
Baseball season
I'm lonely, sandy, and wet
Then finally
Kids, umps, bats, gloves, and helmets are finally done
It's baseball season
I'm going to get hit
And thrown over and over again
Then once you know it, it's the end of the season.

Ocean
by Kylee Kelchner

As you lie in the sun
You listen to the sound of waves
That soar upon the ocean floor
To crash upon the dusty shore
Filled with color, the shells
Float to shore and rescued by
Happy little fingers
Of kids filled with joy
Then when the fun is done
You wake to find the
Enormous setting sun

Spring Is Here
by Kevin Jefferson

Spring is here!!
Hearing birds chirping back and forth,
Like humans having a conversation.
Smelling the fresh cut grass,
Letting you know spring is here.
Sitting outside seeing kids playing sports,
And having the sun beat bright on your face.
Spring is here.
We all have a job to do,
We have to keep the Earth clean, and
GREEN!!

I May Be Small
by Phillip Montag

I may be small.
I may not be tall.
But I will always stay strong.
I may be small.
If I was tall, people will realize I'm not small.
If I fall, I won't get hurt because it's not that big of a fall.
I may be small, I could be tall. But maybe I don't want to be tall.
Just because you're tall doesn't make you smarter
So live in my world for one day, you may want to be small then.

Upcycling
by Jhorden Chambers

I love the sound of scissors cutting the fabric.
While the clippings fly into the air.
I feel like the best upcycler in the world.
The sound of the fabric ripping and stretching makes me
feel like I can do anything.
When I go to a thrift shop, I walk out like a boss!
Outside they ask me where I get my clothes,
They're surprised when I say, "I made it myself!"

Birds
by Owen Barclay

Birds, vivid, colorful, small or big, fast or slow.
Birds, thousands of different birds out there
They can be from any size or any shape
Any color, any sound
The sounds are like something you have never heard before
The chirps and screams
And the songs are like no song before
They are all different in a way
They communicate in their own language
There are two genders, girl and guy
If birds can fly why oh why can't I ...

Basketball
by Immanuel Maro

Running, playing, jumping, shooting,
Passing, bouncing, yelling, doing.
I could feel the hard ball, I could hear the cheering crowd,
I could see other players running all around.
Basketball is fun to play
But when I lose, I practice all day.
I love basketball this I know,
But when I grow up, I hope to become a pro.
Since I can't be pro now, I will wait until I grow up,
But I will keep on practicing to be in the starting lineup.

The End of the Tunnel
by Lilly Leonowitz

When people tell you it gets better,
in the middle of a dark time,
you tend to think they're lying.
There's no way that there's a ray of sunshine
at the end of this dark tunnel.
Engulfed in hideous thoughts of hatred and despair,
ugly and worthless,
untalented.
Numb,
wanting only to feel.
Dread and pain,
both inside and out.
Becoming reclusive,
hiding within myself.
But as it turns out,
what they say is true.
With the end of every storm comes a shimmering rainbow.
Happy days return, full of laughter and shining smiles.
And I am left stronger,
with battle scars left for proof.

Sea Salt
by Grace Li

I hear the dull click of metal kissing metal,
as the door closes and the stairs fall silent.
Are you asleep Father?
My voice uncertain like the salty seas.
Remember ... Remember when we set out against the bitter winds,
as we cast in our line?
As the relentless winds battered our vessel,
and we reeled in salmon as pink as our faces specked with salt.
Do you remember Father? I receive no answer.
Father?
You lie prostrate, your face as calm as the afternoon ocean
bathed in sunlight.
Father I am here.
Let us return to the ocean,
let the waves carry us out to sea,
but Father, I never knew that the sea could taste so salty.

Analysis of Football
by Cooper Davis

It's all about the score, it's all about the game.
All about the money, and all about the fame.
You might fumble the ball the whole time,
You might intercept, I'll bet you a dime.
You'll get hit, you'll get beat.
It's all about the movement of your feet.
The ball will date the air, 5 seconds or more.
If not, you'll be dumped to the floor.
It's all about the score, the game,
The money and the fame!

Skinny
by Madison Wynn

She stares at herself in the mirror
Wishing she could be skinny for once
Wanting to fit in with the girls at school
Striving to be thin even if it kills her
Her mother calls her daughter to dinner,
Oblivious that she has different ideas
She screams into her pillow, shouting into an empty void,
But no one answers, all there is to blame is the oppressive grip of society
She struggles with the fact that she'll never be the perfect image of the perfect girl
And when she's slowly fading away,
Society will say that they've claimed another one.

Skating
by Sanara Windless

I love skating,
And wind blowing in my face.
I love falling,
Because I know the more you fall the better you become.
I love helping little kids, so that they won't fall.
I love watching everyone have fun.
I love hearing the music coming from the DJ booth.
I love when they turn off the lights.
I love speeding through everyone.
I love meeting friends in the cafeteria,
So we can catch up.
I love feeling free when I skate.

The Competition
by Nakita Guiteau

All around me I see people talking
But all I hear is my heart
From the diving board all I see is the calm blue water
Three ... two ... one Pow! Splash! I'm off!
I dive in and taste the chlorine
All I see is water for miles and miles
My arms and feet pumping as fast as my heart
Faster and faster until I reach the wall
I backstroke and look up at the clouds
I dream that I'm swimming through outer space
Boom! I hit my head against the wall like a tennis ball hits a racket
My dream disappears like smoke into the air
"Bye bye pool," I say, "I'll see you next time."
With my medal in my hands.

Anything
by Theresa Perez

The hardest part of this poem for me,
Is finding a topic, can't you see?
This poem can be about whatever I want,
A book, or a movie, or even a restaurant.
But I think I want something a bit more exciting,
So please, help me out, I'm inviting!
Things dash through my mind like cheetahs on the run,
Now wouldn't that be a whole lot of fun!
But ugh! I just don't know what I'll write about,
In my brain it's all just one big blackout!
Anything, anything, why, why, why?
This pressure is killing me, my creativity's run dry!
Maybe I'll write about dragons or magic,
But my time's running out! Tick tick tick!
My topic, ugh! What should it be?
Why did this have to happen to me?
The hardest part of this poem for me,
Is finding a topic, can't you see?
But as I look down at my paper now,
I realize, Anything can be my topic! Wow!

The Four Seasons
by Jake Spingler

The flowers are growing
The breeze is blowing
It's not hot yet
So no need to fret
Everything is just flowing
You can feel the sand
It's in your hand
The water feels great
It doesn't get dark until eight
There are some great bands
The leaves are falling
Kids are calling
School is back
People are back on track
There is no more stalling
The snow is coming
The kids are humming
Christmas songs
Kids get toys except for ones with wrongs
But there is no running ...

Seasons
by Gabrielle Wheeler

Springtime is,
When flowers start to grow.
In the summer months is,
When I will start to mow.
Summer is hot and sunny
But it's my favorite time of the year,
Because it's not muddy.
With fall fast approaching
I've got to get my butt in gear,
With raking leaves and picking up sticks.
Winter is here,
It's cold and windy but with plenty of firewood,
The smoke rolls out the chimney.
It's warm and toasty in this house,
This bitter winter season,
I complained about splitting firewood,
But at least I'm not freezin'.

Regret
by Adria Arbogast

Have you ever felt that feeling
When your stomach is in pain?
Crying out, knowing something bad has happened?
Not the stabbing, piercing pain,
The aching 'curl up in a ball' pain,
Or even the 'punched in the stomach' pain.
It's the pain where it feels as though it is sinking,
Sinking as quickly as a poorly crafted paper boat.
The pain has a name.
Regret.
Anyone can summon it
By saying something they shouldn't have.
Many people know how to avoid regret,
But in the heat of the moment,
Your knowledge is defenestrated.
For those who don't know how to avoid regret,
It's simple.
Think before you act.

Spring
by Ziwen Zhou

Winter is departed
And Earth has lost its glistening white sheets
The awakened sun thaws the tender earth
So it may give a sacred birth
To those that have been entombed
And it is true, nothing is as beautiful as spring
When the wild grass shoots through the ground, lovely and lush
It marks the time of life anew
Heard first is the tenor thrush, singing its melody for all to enjoy
Striking the ear like a dash of lightning
The trees leaf and bloom, yearning toward the sky so blue
The sky will turn a deathly black to unleash a storm so fierce
Torrents and torrents of rain crashing down
Fuel for the many that live below
It is the time for the throwing off of the chains
Everyone may enjoy spring carefree
Ready to live another day
In a beautiful, just world

Childhood
by Amanda Marley

Can we go back to the days
All the way back to May
When we were way too little
To know what we were going to be
After we were all grown up
We have such a boring life now
Like we are going to die
The clouds are all gray
The sun hides away
The flowers are drooping
The sun used to smile
The clouds would be floating
The trees would dance with the breeze
When we were so little
We used to play all day
Like there was no night
Just day

When Will Summer Be Here?
by Joel Shane

From September 'til June
I am consumed
By books, tests, and papers.
They devour my time
Whether it's rain or shine
Fall, winter, spring, forever.
When will summer be here?
I long for sunny days
With brilliant rays
That hug and warm my body.
Instead I am stuck here
For most of the year
Like gum stuck to a shoe.
When will school be over?
It doesn't seem fair
That I have to be here
Nine months out of twelve.
I'd rather sleep in late
Oh, I cannot wait!
When will summer be here?

Sports
by Jordan Hughes

4th down and the score is tied
Game 7 is on the line
Full count and bases loaded
Waiting on the starting block
Ready to dive in the pool
Match point to win the tournament
A header will get the goal
Snapshot goes past the goalie
This is sports
Sports are like life
There are ups and downs
Sports are the most exciting thing in the world
The yelling and clapping of the crowd is the best part
Don't give up, even on the last play
This is sports

Unknown and Alone
by Alex Worrall

You saw the animals had been beaten
You heard them cry
You made them better
You helped them get by
You were gentle
As gentle as can be
For these poor animals
Were through more than you or me
They were starved
And beaten too
They didn't know it was wrong
They had no clue
They only knew
They were in so much pain
They hurt so much
And then you came
They either went to their new owners
And their happiness had shown
Or they had died
And remained unknown and alone

Guitar
by Nathan Thompson

Gradually getting better
Unique and explored
Initial instrument was lute
Terrific harmonics
Amazing sounds
Ready to be played

Basketball
by Tommy Buchert

I watched as jealousy haunted over me
As he bounded the ball on the Boone basketball court
That should be me down there
But I didn't go all out in tryouts
Which cost me the spot
Basketball is my life
So next year
I will try my hardest
to make the team
And accomplish my dream

Dream
by Kitiara Crosby

As I rest my head on my pillow,
I wait, and wait for that lovely fellow,
who every night comes and shares adventures and stories
of things that have yet to come, of which history will bellow.
I dream of cats that can fly
I dream of dogs that sleep in tights
I dream of birds that can't fly
I dream of oceans without tides
I dream of horses without manes
I dream of mice with canes
I dream of fire that doesn't burn
I dream of cows that talk about birds
I dream of ice which does not melt
I dream of hope

Happiness
by Miracle Ruiz

Happily ever after
All or nothing
Precious love
Pure heart
Interesting thoughts
Never give up
Endless possibilities
Sweet dreams
Special occasion

Don't Be Annoying
by Zachary Sabold

My brother and sister are so annoying
My brother and sister are so annoying that my ears explode
My brother and sister are so annoying that their voices play on and on in my head
My brother and sister are so annoying that you can hear them from a mile away
My brother and sister are so annoying that they are in the world records book
for the most annoying kids on the planet

Snowflakes
by Megan Kidd

I am a snowflake.
I fall from the sky slowly unto the ground.
I am one of a kind.
I am tiny, and microscopic.
Many believe I am soft.

I am a snowflake.
I travel down with many other snowflakes.
We are all different.
When we join together as one, we become a blanket of snow.
I don't feel very alone then, in fact, I am with millions of other snowflakes.
I feel this sense of great joy when children of all shapes and sizes take my friends
And build them into snowmen.
When I see such a sight, I wait to be played with, like a toy.
I watch the children walk past, hour after hour, until sundown.
Then I start to feel alone again.
I think to myself, although surrounded by thousands of other snowflakes.
But deep inside a murky forest with some ray of light,
I truly am alone.

Seeds
by Brian Soriano

We are all seeds
who get blown around
Until we heed
Resources that abound
With someone we love
we plant our roots
And grow up to
the skies above
As our flowers blossom and bloom
New life emerges in a shimmering plume
Of seeds, which take their turn to blow
Across the wind to take root and grow

Lost and Alone
by William Gill, Brendan O'Neal, and Edward Ochanas

It causes me pain on the inside and out
There's a hero within me who just wants to shout.
An ugly person with no heart or pride
Has problems much bigger than mine
Which it has chosen to hide
It calls me names such as "weird" or "fat"
If I tell, they'll yell names at me like "snitch" or "rat"
It's the emotional stress I can bear no longer
But as the cliché goes, "What doesn't kill you makes you stronger"
Today is the day that I must tell
A teacher or guardian about this living hell
I take the long way to my cubby
To avoid the verbal abuse like, "dumb" and "chubby"
I walked into my classroom and spotted the teacher
I was about to tell the words of truth just like a preacher
She looked at me in shock and awe
This bully's reign of terror is about to fall
As she called his name I felt complete
For this bully felt defeat

3rd
Place

Eleanor Wikstrom

Prophecy
by Eleanor Wikstrom

Past windows of filth where light struggles to breach
On a floor where hatred and turned heads
have bred cruel markings of 'the greater good'
Lies a woman under the deep sleep of oppression.
Ubiquitous on her skin is a barcode that lets the others know she's hopeless
In her dreams she calls out to the family she's lost
and wonders how she can get them back.
She remembers the forks in the road for opportunity
that were always closed when she reached them
A taunt that turned into bullying, bullying that turned into reality,
reality that turned into a dream.
The belaying rope snapped before she could reach the top
Hidden, like a diseased child, she awaits for a time to escape her bounds
Reveal her ferocious roar, a roar of injustice, lost chances, and a leader's fear.
To regain what she lost in a land where all the doors are closed
Possibility a Heaven that she will reach.
A woman, the unwanted meal of the justice system
Phosphorescent, shuddering with anticipation, smelling eternity
Prophecy.

2nd Place

Allison Regenwether

Fear
by Allison Regenwether

He was disgusting;
His nails grotesque and long as they raked through my hair;
His breath horrid as he breathed down my neck;
Close your eyes;
take a deep breath;
Open those eyes, but he's still there;
He's always there;
Always waiting, always watching;
Ready to pounce at any second;
Whispering as I shake;
Persuading me to quit;
To join him;
It would be easy, oh, easy would be nice;
His voice dripped with malign as his words grew;
Louder;
Louder in my head;
I step forward;
His voice fades;
I clear my throat, I feel proud;
But he's always there, always watching.

1st
Place

Ann Zhang

One of the most powerful pieces we had the pleasure of judging
came from 6th grade student, Ann Zhang.
It wasn't surprising to hear that when she isn't doing homework,
this talented young lady spends most of her time writing short stories.
She also has an interest in French
and continues to study the language as her busy schedule permits.
Ann aspires to be a teacher one day, and we wish her much success.

Nostalgia
by Ann Zhang

In a disgraced and polluted city
near the old orphanage, where he grew up
the old man lives in half a cardboard box
and as they walk by they taunt him; tease his muddied clothes,
the crooked way he walks
Their words become the wood to the fire of his suffering
But my dear, burning takes time, and he lives, not dead but dying
No one knows the old man's name
they blow smoke into the air and explode with laughter around him
they shatter bottles of alcohol against the sidewalks
But despite their wretched doings, the old man gives
He gives every last bit of his life and pours it into those around him
He fills the empty hearts of the children,
when their father is drunk in the cellar
and their mother ran off to some boyfriend's party
He expects nothing in return for his tender deeds
The old man makes us wonder why we, those who have so much
cry in vain over such lesser things, so blind and ignorant
and those with empty pockets have fuller hearts
and love with more honesty than we could ever buy
Today, I think wistfully of the old man
as I throw a bitter rose onto his grave

Division III

Grades
8-9

No More Worrying
by Amber Mooney

A child abandoned
Taken in but never kept
Wondering, "What's wrong with me."
Never given a chance
Never loved by anyone
Always thought she was alone
Until one day
The love for that child
Will show
And that child would
Not have to worry anymore
So no more will that child
Be abandoned or not loved.

Imagination
by Nancy McGrath

I have a pet leprechaun, his name is Song.
He's small and frail,
With curly red hair and a smile that reaches Hong Kong.
He's friendly and cute and loves to tell a tall tale.
Meet my fairy, her name is Cumberland.
She's my very best friend,
And we fly high in the sky to her homeland.
She will be mine till the very end.
I lost my leprechaun today.
Mother says that he left with Cumberland.
I guess it was time for them to go away,
But how I wish they were here in my hand.
Today is my sixth birthday.
Nothing special, just another day.
Mom is out, Dad is gone, nobody to say hurray!
Song is gone and so is Cumberland, nobody to save the day.
When I wake up the next day something is wrong.
My friends never reappears, yet it's okay.
I know know that I will never be as young
As I was when I played with Song.
Oh how I wish I figured this out yesterday.

Run, Forrest, Run
by Dale Victor C. Glova

The girl said, "Run, Forrest, run!"
And the boy ran, and ran
Like a bullet, lightning quick,
Just like a speeding man.
But the run wasn't for fun,
for he was being chased.
And young Forrest ran, and ran
With the most lithe and haste
The chasers in question were
three young, troublesome boys
who were fast, fearsome tigers
on bikes and with much noise.
The sprinter was a cheetah,
down roads, by moving cars,
through large fields and football fields,
past loud drinkers in bars.
Now, talking to his mother,
aft'r escaping with cunning,
he said, "Now, wher'er I'm goin'
I'm always a-running!"

Just a House On Maple Street
by Skylar Lacey

On the outside, I stand so tall
Brightening the street in which I stand
My garden has just been updated for the spring
And my windows have just been Windexed
Two cars will leave but always return to my long, curved driveway
My garage will occasionally open too
I am a brown and maroon 3-D square
I look so quiet and peaceful as I stand at the back of Maple Street
On the inside, five children's footprints wildly roam the house
A crazy dog runs in circles around the living room
Toys are constantly being left behind as a baby crawls around
There are sounds of laughs and good times while the family eats dinner
The chaotic times of the family is what makes it fun
The stains of the carpet in the playroom remind me
that I'm lived in by a crazy family of seven
Every day their life seems to be filled with more joy as they all grow together
On the outside, I may look plain, but on the inside, I am certainly not

Peace In Mind
by Gabriella Hammer

It is dark and I can't see,
So I close my eyes and I start to dream
I'm portaled there as if by magic
To a non-existent place
There I soar high in the sky
With feathery wings that let me fly
Enchanted by a magical view
As the stars twinkle above
When I land at a glassy blue lake,
The crack of dawn is in my wake
An orange crescent slides over the land
And shocking color stains the night
I dive deep into the lake
Trying to avoid the cognizance of day
But the cold is like a slap in the face
Then, suddenly, I am awake

Lost In the Wild
by Nicole Weber

The birds chirp and the river is tricklin',
The animals hide in the green leaves.
The trees start to sway in the raging storm,
In the strong, hard winds, they seem to breathe.
A girl staring back at the evil eyes,
A stick in her hand held like a bat.
Stuck with wearing her old raggedy clothes,
Not even knowing how to attack.
There is one rustling of a small bush.
The girl jolts back, scared out of her mind.
Not even knowing what else to do,
She runs, leaving all the creatures behind.
A black bear is staring into her eyes.
It had eyes that are as dark as night.
He snarls, exposing his bright, white teeth.
She stands completely still, scared out of fright.
Her feet are planted into the ground.
The bear is confused and backs away.
She stands taller than a skyscraper.
As proud as she feels, she cannot stay.

Darts ...
by Suhmer Gantt

Pricking me, sticking me, stabbing me, jabbing me
The pain of malicious words
penetrated my skin.
I ran away, weeping on the inside.
Believing the poison darts stuck in my heart
As I stared at me staring back at me
I asked myself
What do I see?
My eyes, my nose, my teeth are just right
My skin, my hair, there's nothing wrong there
As I concentrated on what's good about me
The pain began to ease, I began to breathe
And the darts, those poison darts, dropped to the floor
I crushed them under my feet, crushed them to dust
Determined to never let them touch me again
Because I realized I like who I am.
I like being me
And from the depth of me,
I'll be the best me I can be

These Four Walls of Anxiety
by Kaitlyn Hess

These four walls are made of stone; permanent.
Their cold façade is molded by my fears.
I try to fight but have no armaments.
These walls are too strong; for that I shed tears.
They surround me, taking all my ardor.
I cry out for help, but it is not heard.
I compromise, but they snub my barter.
I fear the suffocation is incurred.
One of these days, these four walls will crumble.
Knowing this gives me a glimmer of hope.
The way this will happen leaves me fumbled.
Until that day, I'm learning how to cope.
I'm the lone one who can break these four walls;
For my fear keeps them from foreshadowed falls.

Society
by Ben McCormick

Society is a brainwashed place,
With so many faults.
Telling people what they can and cannot do.
And even what and who they can't be.
Society is a diseased place,
Filled with thousands of stereotypes.
People everywhere afraid to embrace themselves.
And we act and talk like others want us to.
Society is a pathetic place.
We are told to be ourselves,
But when we are,
We are shunned upon.
Society is a broken place.
Crumbling cities and homeless people,
Suicide and abuse.
Why can't anyone see that society is a truly and utterly brainwashed place?

Joyful Summer
by Caitlyn Kwiatkowski

Joy is summer,
It fills you with warmth
And makes you smile,
The little kids play
But it's not here to stay,
The warmth fades away
And so does the light,
The kids get sad,
But don't you worry
It'll be back in a hurry,
When it's gone
You're cold and upset
Just don't fret
Because all good things must come to an end,
Soon it will be just within reach
And the smile comes back upon your face,
The kids go back out
And the birds sing again,
The bees will buzz
And the light is back.

Children Are Flowers
by Isabelle Geiger

Children are flowers,
always growing.
They love it outside,
petals petting green grass,
leaves dancing in the rain.
Children are flowers,
making people smile,
making happy babies bounce,
spreading joy to everyone.
Children are flowers,
and when they bloom,
they show their colors,
by dancing around,
while smiles grew on the faces watching.

Struck Through the Heart
by Angelique Conti

When at first we met, 'twas not yet love
A feeling I could not explain
It was a match destined to be
Fell upon me like a light rain
His kisses tender like a dove
Words spoken softly with such depth
This intimacy new to me
His warmth left on my breath
Promises our life everlasting
No other shall be the same
He's drawn like a canvas to art
Where some have gone, he will remain
Temptation circles him like a ring
A feeling takes him by surprise
How another girl stole his heart
Tears well up within my sad eyes
My heart is heavy, how could this be
Promises shattered by this girl
Wake me up from this awful nightmare
I'm lost and broke from this love whirl.

The Wine of Age
by Abigail Rowan

Some people dread the 'growing up'
It seems so cruel to soul and mind
And yet it fills the heavenly cup
With pints and pints of lovely wine.
And still some people seem to think
That grapes are sweeter than the wine.
And yet do grapes mature with age,
Ripen, blossom over time?
Why no, grapes don't have that potential.
They only change in bodily shape.
For when they get all dried and wrinkled
Raisins take the place of grapes.
So do not cling to passing time,
Life is a sweet but brief occasion.
And may your grapes be turned to wine
Instead of ugly wrinkled raisins.

Little Did Those People Know
by Brianna Particelli

It was a beautiful morning
In the city of New York.
But little did those people know
That tragedy soon would show.
Some folks were on their way to work
Thinking that they would be fine.
In those two towers standing tall,
But those towers soon would fall.
When the nation watched the planes hit,
Their hearts were filled with much pain.
The painful rage tore them apart
Like a knife was in their heart.
The sound of people screaming
Was louder than explosions.
The smoke that lingered in the air
Was like something that could scare.
When the towers fell on that day
People held onto their lives.
But little did those people know,
That they would have to let go.

The Ladder Meant For Me
by Rachael Martin

Whoa! I'm trapped
Trapped in a big midnight black rectangular kind of prison cell.
All I see, while watching, is this big ladder as tall as a white pine tree,
being lowered down to me.
Why?
How did I even get in here?
The only thing I smell is the fresh pine wood scent on the ladder,
that is being handed down to me.
All I see is this ladder.
It's meant for me.
I'm going to get out of here.

My Farm Family
by Kyle Milligan

My family is a working farm.
My mom is the boss,
Telling us what to do and how to do it.
My sister is the tractor, big and slow moving.
My dad is the cow, making a mess everywhere and always in the way.
I am the barn that keeps us all together and dry.
That makes us a friendly farm family.

Butterfly
by Arianna Silvano

My sister is a butterfly,
She was in a small cocoon.
All alone and shy,
With no one near to notify.
Now she is a butterfly!
So beautiful and free.
She spread her wings and flew,
And now she's better than me.
You cannot kill her confidence,
Her personality truly shines.
She's passionate about who she is,
That really is no crime.

The Field of Dreams
by Derick Wartzenluft

It was a balmy day.
I showed up at the park.
The place near was a bay.
All I heard were barks.
We took the field together.
We started taking BP and infield on the field.
I thought we were together for forever.
Finally the dogs healed.
I took the plate to bat.
I hit the ball a mile.
They were practicing diving on a mat.
My first BP was filed.
This was the weirdest game,
but everybody came.

A Piece of Asteria
by Amy Viall

Do I shine extra bright?
Or am I just another star,
Splashed into the night?
Will I guide you home,
Or do you just see me as a bunch?
Please; look at me; alone.
Not just another piece of your constellation,
Crying inside,
For an explanation.
Glistening I am,
As you stare at me,
Wide eyed as can be.
I fade away,
A distant memory.
You saw me once,
Then turned around.
Here I am,
But I won't be found.
I am just a star,
But I am already much too far.

How I Feel
by Sunni Holland

This is so exciting,
But so scary at the same time.
He looks like him,
But does he think like him?
This has flipped my world around.
I don't know how to react.
Nobody understands how I feel.
Is this good for the good,
Or for the bad?

Self Portrait
by Nathaniel Solomon

My brown skin is like a new unwrapped tootsie roll.
My ears are as sharp as a moonlight wolf howling.
My lips as smooth as the first slice on Thanksgiving Day.
My flattop is as high as the American flag on the moon.
My heart holds weeds always cut down.
It's as pink as October.
I live in basketball and eat the dunk.

The Dreamer In Me
by Ashley Beasley

I always knew I was fly
My mama always told me I could reach the sky
She took away the cry
When I was shy
And then she took away the pain in no gain
But I never really know why I could go so high
In spite of all the haters
In spite of all the drama
I knew I had to put a comma
And think what Momma said
"I could reach the sky"
I taught myself to aim high
Before it was too late and the Lord told my body to die

Sadness Is an Ocean
by Shanna Zengolewicz

Sadness is an ocean
the ocean is overwhelming
and the tides are strong
as they crash down onto the sandy beach and wash away
sadness is an ocean
the ocean is deep
and filled with so many mysteries
like the mind of one who is miserable
sadness is an ocean
the waves roll off of the shore
like the tears roll off of your cheek
and the fish try and escape their predators
like you try and escape sadness
sadness is an ocean
and it will surely knock you down
and the currents will pull you under
and leave you helpless as you drown
the same way that sadness does

Unwind
by Gianna Tischler

When insecurities
Get the best
And your friendships
Are put to the test,
Don't worry your pretty little mind.
Things,
eventually,
Will unwind.
So when you are in a rut
And you feel like you might be stuck,
Stop moving,
And think it through,
It will all unwind for you.
And when I'm lost, with nowhere to go
I don't sit around and mope
I work it out and cope
Because I know things will unwind
For me and for you.

Field of Crows
by Amanda Blumenstein

A crow sat in a field.
He was fully healed.
No one knew why,
He stayed until he died.
I too now know,
Why he did not go.
It is peaceful and quiet.
There will never be a riot.
Another crow has come.
I don't know what he will become.
Will he stay or go?
No one will ever know.

Decisions
by Victoria Mattis

A young girl wakes up in the morning.
With a decision she has to make.
Will she let the baby live.
Or will its life she take?
Alone unwed and very scared.
She knows the trouble she'll face.
But somewhere down within her heart.
She knows the life inside her cannot be replaced.
She knows God makes each child individually.
And she wonders what the future will be.
Blue-eyed boy or blue-eyed girl.
A couple of months to go until she sees.
Finally she has the little baby.
And as she looks into her eyes.
She accepts her decision, even the hard times ahead.
But that no baby deserves to die.
The choice she made was a hard one.
With her little girl always in sight.
She never regrets her decision.
And now fights for unborn rights.

Imagine If ...
by Mikayla Levkulic

Imagine what the world would be like,
if everyone cared and all were nice.
Imagine the friends you'd have,
and the new people you'd meet.
Imagine the words you would hear,
and the person you could become.
Imagine the help you'd get,
and the advice you'd receive.
No one would be an outcast,
and no one would be called strange.
Everyone would be different,
in a good way.
Imagine people leaving their doors open,
instead of locking them at night.
Imagine a world where children can play,
without any type of fear.
Imagine a place where everyone could be trusted,
where generosity would spread like wildfire.
Imagine what the world would be like,
if everyone cared and all were nice.

Friendship
by Isabel Tobin

It is hard to find the perfect friend
But somehow you will know if you have acquired one
They will stay with you around every bend
When you are feeling like a cloud, they come around and are your sun
You share experiences with them that you will never share with another
You both carry each other's secrets and when they have a new one
you are always the first to learn
They know your limits and with their care you will never smother
Having friends is something that everyone deserves
but best friends are things you must earn
When you have a best friend you jump with them on their bed
until it makes a cracking noise so you stop
You have movie nights and buy popcorn and multiple bags of candy
You and your best friend are always laughing together
until you think you are going to pop
Friendship is accidentally wearing matching clothing and thinking that it's dandy
It takes some time to develop a best friend
But once you do the joy, happiness, laughter, and care will never end

Come Back
by Alyx Berryman

You lied.
You said you would never leave me.
You said we would be together forever.
You were the one, the one who kept me going.
You made me happy, like no one else could.
I still remember last time I saw you,
You told me that you were leaving,
And you would be back soon.
But soon later, a soldier came up to my door,
I knew what he was here to tell me.
As I started to cry,
He said you were gone, forever.
I told him he's wrong,
That you were still out there, fighting.
I didn't want to believe it, believe that you're gone.
I cried for days, not wanting to see the truth.
How can the one I love be gone so fast?
I didn't understand, and I still don't.
It was hard to go on without you, and it still is.
But I still believe you will come back, one day.

Green and Blue
by Tiffany Serra

Green and blue become one
Yellow evades the green
leaving brown
the deep coral is human nature
what's left?
A crumbing home?
Toxic waste?
Nothing.
we destroyed it
now what?
we fly our ships to new lands?
sleep below ground?
This is where we are heading,
we need change
But,
who will?
no one cares
that we are losing our home

I Am
by Yohan Yoo

I am a child
I am a student
I am a citizen
I am an American
I am a human
I am an existence
I am one memory of this time

Tragedy At a Marathon
by Ashley Padayatil

On a bright and beautiful day
The sun rises in the east
The people are making their way
As the birds start making sound
Families are coming to stay
The runners are like wild beasts
Going to walk and run away
Lots of lives will turn around
There was dark smoke that was all gray
It all turned into a creased
And made everyone run to sway
But people fell to the ground
Everyone helped and obeyed
There were not many deceased
The runners and people did say
They found the person around
They did not have any delay
All the people were released
The world we live in is not gray
No one will ever repay

A Generation
by Brianna Chambellan

Where the internet can ruin you, a friend will humiliate you
Importance of knowledge has not found you,
Success will never occur to you
Failure is something that knows you, a book can destroy you
Modern technology will fuel you, no one will remember you
Money does not make you, God made you
So swallow your pride, make Him proud
Turn things around, make changes for the better
And then you will be a trendsetter

I'm Sorry
by Katelyn Gilbert

You are broken
You are hurt
I understand
But you hurt others
Make others broken
That I don't understand
You are a foggy sunrise
You are a mystery
I may be complicated
But you are tangled
I can't help
As much as I try
I can't help
You're like a broken tennis net
I keep trying to fix
With duct tape and frail thread
I'm sorry
I couldn't fix you,
World
But it's gonna be okay

Her
by Cyrus Carlin

Her hair sparkles in the bright sunlight.
Her laugh is heartwarming.
And her looks are charming and beautiful and sweet
I just wish she knew that's what I think
she's the most wonderful, beautiful person alive.
I wish I could talk to her more and be with her more
every minute I'm not with her it feels like ten years
every day I'm not with her it feels like a hundred years.
I can't wait to talk to her again and be around her again
and most of all hear her voice again.

Dreaming
by Grace Thompson-Rhodes

As the sun resigns for the day,
The milkiness of the moon seeps out of a never ending
Pit of darkness.
Filled with hopes and dreams
That will one day come true.
As the darkness creeps up on you,
You're enveloped completely
In an aura of calmness;
A different world,
Where mistakes and hatred all fade away.
Looking up at the sky,
Stars twinkle and shine bright.
Giving you all the strength you need for the night.
You tuck away fears, sadness, and rage.
And lock them in a box,
Throwing away the key.
So you may dream a few dreams
Tonight.
Of things that you long for,
Or things that you need.
You dream of happiness,
Sadness,
And all things imaginable.
But when you wake in the morning,
With the sun shining bright,
You have only distant memories,
From the previous night.

The Darkened Division
by Lauren Saylor

Never love a light, for it never lasts
Darkness deserves the reward of love
It beholds mystery, wonderings
We naturally are attracted to things
That behold the power of hope
Though at a young age, we are taught to be sure
No maybe, only yes or no
Though every day we have a median, a line
Placed in the gray area between what is light
And what is darkness
We never thought of it in a deeper form
Other than useless or useful
Not being the treacherous dark tunnel
Or the light at the end
For it is the journey through the dark tunnel
And the discovery of light at the end
Life ...

Cold Winter's Night
by Emily Campbell

The wind howls on a cold winter's night
Children all tucked up in their warm beds
Not knowing what is just out of sight.
The child awakens from a stomp with might
He looks up to see only but the top of a head,
The wind howls on a cold winter's night.
He creeps his head out of the covers in such terrifying fright
Suddenly a man appears who looks as if he bled,
Not knowing what is just out of sight.
The man picks him up with great force and says everything will be all right;
He fights but the man throws him far instead,
The wind howls on a cold winter's night.
He begs and pleads but the man won't tell tonight.
"Mister, where am I going, I'm scared," he says,
Not knowing what is just out of sight.
To a place where everything will be a delight,
And the milk cartons are no longer read;
The wind howls on a cold winter's night
Not knowing what is just out of sight.

My War
by Jordan Grace

Walking onto the battlefield
As ready as could be
All I see are fallen comrades
And old friends all bloody
They never gave up
And so death took their lives
But I will fight for my fallen comrades
Because they would for me

Sunset
by Alexis Blanchette

The colors paint the one blank canvas that we call the sky.
Each color is a brushstroke, each unique in their own way.
The colors fade together, they mix, and they blend.
The color drifts away taking the dreams many people shared.
Their dreams go to Heaven, where it is always day,
But here on Earth it's dark now, the day has faded away.

Goodbye
by Kristin Harritt

Nothing lasts forever,
I knew the time was here.
It was something I didn't want to endeavor.
I wanted to believe it was never,
I wish I could disappear.
Nothing lasts forever.
Family is a treasure,
Losing them is a feeling so clear.
It was something I didn't want to endeavor.
It was like my heart was severed.
It encased me in a wave of fear.
Nothing lasts forever.
I wasn't ready whatsoever.
I wouldn't see them for years.
It was something I didn't want to endeavor.
What if I didn't see them again ever?
Then they saddled into their army gear.
Nothing lasts forever.
It was something I didn't want to endeavor.

Looking Glass
by Samantha Pontier

The looking glass that you see from
Might have a glare of the sun
You enjoying life is such a lie
I see right through your bright disguise
Still, the looking glass that I see through
Never reveals a happy you
You act like you are just fine
True feelings will reveal in due time
Life's battles are not always won
So take advantage of any joy and fun
The finer things in life only come
To those who know how to get to them
Dark souls always need to fight
To find a way into the light
The looking glass that you see from
Needs to let you out into the sun

Ocean Shore
by Lexi Wheeler

The islands are the heart
and soul of the sea
specific to their bodies
and the beaches are like the flesh,
waves are the emotion
I, like any other, strive
for the warmth of the sun.
"The sand is my paradise,"
says the young man
who lies next to me,
"I am the yearning for the heat
all humans desire."
Any woman who can desire
the fire in any soul of man
is the woman of human nature
she is the dame I strive for,
she is the role I must take up.
Though I may be small in this big universe of mine,
but my heart must take the lead
towards the shore.

The Lost Dreamer
by Selena Quintanilla

She was the nightmare
when everything fell apart
at the time her life was transformed
for the first time
she learned what it was like to be a part of something
larger and deeper than herself to appreciate the blessings
all she had to do was watch
it was everywhere
in the look ... in the touch ... in the laughter
she dared to dream of a better life
a love of her own
this can be yours
the wind sang as a promise
then everything
changed

Cry
by Sophia Swartz

I breathe deep breaths
Like thunderclaps, they resonate.
Deep, hiccupping, earthquakes that
Shake, uproot, and fracture,
Like someone ripped the world apart,
Took my world, shredding it down the middle
With hairline incisions
Branching out like leafy boughs.
The earthquake comes with boiling rains,
Scorching torrents streaking balmy paths
On my skin that will never leave,
The memory that shall never die;
My immortal inner tempest.
My body quakes as though
You are shaking me, brandishing me,
And I can hear your battle cry
Through the earthly tremors and unrelenting rains,
Your fury embodied in your racking screams,
My penance embodied in my quiet absolution.
Please– I may only ask for solitude when I cry.

Music Fills the Soul
by Mikala Hardie

Music is the thing that keeps us going
When everything all around us has failed;
It is like a warm, summer breeze blowing
Comforting us when everyone has bailed.
Music fills us, with life and joy and hope,
It's a way to forget everything,
And when we listen, it helps us to cope
It's no wonder it makes us want to sing.
When you put on a song and close your eyes,
The world disappears all you have is peace,
The birds start to sing, the sun starts to rise,
Happiness surrounds you, all the stress you release.
Life without music is life without glee
Dull and boring and meaningless to me.

Miracles
by Lauren Crim

Hard to grasp
Tough to reach
Impossible to know
Impossible to seek
Catch you by surprise
You can't understand why
Lost in the moment
Unable to speak.
Come when they are needed most
By day or by sleep
Lost in time
Lost in weep
They come for young and old
They come for tired and weak
The job they bring to us
Makes your heart skip a beat
You day can be made
Your day's at its peak
When a miracle comes
And gives you a treat.

The Teenage Fight
by Xandra Coleman

Life at our age is a long continuous brawl
With our hands in a fist we fight all day and we battle all night
We fight to survive, we fight and move on
With the school and the stress, suicides and self harm
We have no time to waste, no none at all
Survival of the fittest that is what it is called
The bullies and self serving will be the ones to learn to strike first
While the quietly strong just pick up their scars and try to hang on
We fight day and night, without any lessons, just one step at a time
Dizzy from the punch, we stumble along,
Wondering when exactly this fight had begun
We listen to shouts from the sidelines
That let us know we can't give up or lose the fight
Although not everyone can win, yes some will fall,
Fall and not get up, for them the fight is done
Those who bet on the fallen will hand in the money, upset and confused
So sure that their person would win, they were strong, what went wrong?
Their defense weakens, fists loosen, now the better must fight
Will they win? Will they fall?
Life as a teenager isn't easy, no not at all
We fight day and night to survive, to move on

Misconceptions and False Assumptions
by Isabella Galante

We live in a world of poor assumptions
our bones which seem hardy
I compare to the fragileness of a daisy
butterflies in our stomachs
which can indeed feel more as killer bees
sometimes I think the moon controls the waves
more than our brain controls us
and the words spilled across the page
come from the heart more than the hand writing them
many things we would be told to know
are most often to be incorrect assumptions
funny isn't it?

For Me Defined
by Princess Ladson-Rahman

The title American has a history
A pained monster lurking
alone under society's bed
For me you see was no walk
'twas genocide's asleep, sit-downs
imprisonment the ultimate price
for being American
Only for the darkened soil
who dared resemble me
Now, Oh BOY! How about these days
They fought then …
We forfeit now …
I'm ashamed to say
I'm disgraced at what my eyes consume
trickle trickle down effect
We are still enslaved
Oh what it means to be
AMERICAN.

Dance Class
by Drewliana Vann

I get up early in the morning
I wake up to go to dance class
I brush my teeth, then eat breakfast
Put my dance clothes on and do my hair.
I put my sneakers on. And get my stuff together
My mom and I get in the car and drive
I go into dance class then and stretch my legs
The teacher calls us in to go
The dance is slow but then my body moves quickly
I feel alive, excited and little bubbles of joy pop out of me.
In and stretch, the type of things that I do in dance class
My toes point, my legs jump and swing.
The time that I leave dance class is about at least four o'clock
My body is really tired, but I have extra energy
Energy to dance again.

If
by Tina Messner

If the world outside, was as bright as my mind,
Would you know how I live?
If I always had a smile on my face, painted or real,
Would you think there was nothing wrong where I live?
If I go out for a walk, with music in my ears,
Would you think I want to escape from the life I live?
If I were to trip, to fall in my path,
Would you stop to see if I was okay?
If time were to stand still, to have the option to continue or return,
Would you want me to continue?
If life was not seen in colors, only black and white,
Would you want me to see black?
If the sun doesn't shine, and it's leading us through a dark path,
Would you want me to find the light?
If the world outside, was as bright as my mind,
Would I want to change the way I live?

I Am From
by Annie Steinbrink

I am from my Downy smelling lovey, from Jessica McClintock and Grey Flannel
I am from the furry dogs suspended over my head
Breathing, observing, protecting me like a mother with her baby cub
I am from the eavesdropping room,
Freezing like a meat locker
Whose old creaky floor I remember
When trying to be soothed as I cry a blood-curdling cry.
I'm from freshly baked challah and greasy potato latkes, from Abraham to Rachel.
I'm from the Princetons and Penns,
From newly strung Wilson racquets and muddy grass stained Adidas cleats
I'm from the big brown eyes, and cold wet nose,
with sandy blond hair and a heart of pure gold
I'm from Joseph and Estelle,
blood red roast beef and freshly polished spinning table
From the leg my mom lost to the cancer,
The smile my grandfather was powerless to show
Under my roof are family pictures, lingering to tell its stories,
A family of this kind so rich in history,
I am from these moments–
The ones that make me, me–
I now pass it on, l'dor vador

Purple
by Danny Nguyen

Purple
Delicious, juicy grapes, big giant football fish, tasty round plums
Taste of sour cream, smell of a new car, fresh broccoli
Late winter nights
A purple amethyst and a happy person after Christmas, early January
Healthy, tired, excited

Music
by Newosi Silum

Rap, Pop, and Alternative,
Different genres musicians give.
Rock, Country, and R&B,
show me things I couldn't see.
All of my favorite songs,
I play them all night long.
Stop, Shuffle, Replay,
going on every single day.
Even though society divides us,
music somehow seems to unite us.

Emmanuel Uses Me
by Taylor Grant

This relationship won't be forever
I know you love me and I love you too
It won't work and we can't stay together
And my life is so much lost without you
I know I need you and you need the same,
Every wall I built up is crashing down.
You take it lightly but it is no game
But with the crashing I hate the sound.
We're a beautiful nightmare so don't wake me,
My heart bleed black tears of our sexy lust
But sounds of your menacing voice shakes me,
This feeling could be described as unjust
He assures me I won't find anyone better, but I tell him I already have
He asks how sure and I say
Don't the waves pull the sand ...
Don't the moon pull the tide ...

Lunar
by Kylie Procita

Distorted mute noise.
An imaginary soundtrack
blind light blasts through the air
slowly engulfing the spectrum
in sound waves
of motion and suspension.
Coming to grips with the flaming inevitability
the puncture of reality
that the truth is around the corner
but in the present
thinking is the only option,
thoughts are all we have.
They are what sculpt creativity.
What creates minds with
careless imagination.

Travel
by Kaitlyn Osorio

I have never traveled far away.
I know only my small town home.
My body is a solitary object
That stays where it is,
Moving only small distances.
I have never traveled far away,
I know only my small town home.
But I've been to other worlds.
My body is a solitary object
That stays where it is,
But my mind is a wayfaring stranger,
Walking down a never ending trail of fiction.
I have never traveled far away,
But the paper airplane with a million words takes me wherever it desires.
My body is a solitary object, but the sailing ships carrying imaginary lives
Take me across every ocean
Allowing me to live an impossible life in the rectangular pages
that I love to call home.
I have never traveled far away, but the hundreds of stamps
In my passport
Say otherwise.

The Bird
by Josie LaTorres

Do you remember that one bird?
the one in the park,
with feathers the color of your eyes?
the one that sat on the brown branch,
the branch that had those green leaves?
in the park where the children played?
do you remember the wooden benches,
the benches that creaked whenever we sat down?
do you remember the beautiful breeze?
do you remember the brightness of the sky?
do you remember that one bird's wings,
with the beautifully colored feathers,
as they spread and that bird flew–
off the brown branch with the green leaves,
over the children and the wooden benches in the park,
gliding on the beautiful breeze and into the bright sky?
I do.

Only Human
by Sasha Buxo

You know it's funny,
how they say, you don't know how much you love something till you set it free.
Was that how you felt with me?
You let me go, didn't have to think twice.
My life was perfect for 14 years straight until today. Why now?
You come running into my life, expecting me to forgive and forget.
Guess what, I'm only human and it takes time.
But it's funny, how you come unexpectedly and want things from me.
What happened when I was small and I needed things from you?
Why weren't you there when those boys would bully me?
Or when my first softball game came around.
You were supposed to be in the stands, cheering me on, but you weren't!
No, but now that bars are in front of you, you need me the most.
So you know what now, now you can wait!
When you come out
Then you can call me, then you can come to one of my games.
But it's too late, because those boys stopped bullying me.

Zehra (The Lady of Light)
by Alleh Naqvi

The heart speaks the Truth
Reflecting the face of Light
A treasure to find.

Sacrifices
by Erin Albus

Is this really the only answer you have?
Must everyone be brought to their knees?
You have to win, I see that now.
You have to see everyone broken and bloody.
You have be the one to destroy them.
I know what you really are now.
A monster through and through.
You have no morals, no sympathy.
You're barely human, barely there.
I know how to break you,
destroy your nonexistent soul.
I promise you I will have you on your knees.
I will have you begging for your life.
I will have you groveling like you had others.
And you deserve every second of agony.
I may become like you, but I accept my fate.
Sacrifices are needed to win a war,
and I will do just that; I will win this war.

A Painful Truth
by Erika Schofield

Life is not a given, not something that is promised
Life is a present, something to prosper from
Death is a right, inevitable and unstoppable
A force bigger than ourselves
The day we learn not to fear death
Is the day our life truly begins
It's a painful truth, but it keeps us alive
No longer required to tremble in the shadows of our fears
Instead sprouting our wings
Continuing to keep pushing forward
Stronger than you were in the past
Weaker than you'll be in the future

A Forced Poem
by Emily Donovan

The best poetry is natural.
It comes with no warning and pours out onto the page
one thought after another.
One beautiful word flowing out
followed by the next
until there is no way to stop.
The worst poetry is forced.
The words won't come out
but you need them to.
Your thoughts become muddled
into one.
No matter how hard you try
to paint the page with words
it stays blank.

He Holds All Power
by Emily Goulas

He made us with the same two hands we all have today,
covered in soft layered skin with the warmth of the hot buns right out of the oven.
The only thing that is asked every day is selfish things,
when really we have everything he doesn't.
He gives back what was taken by someone who is just jealous of us heavenly kids,
because his powers were taken and formed into the opposite of heavenly.
The way we live is outrageous, when the daffodils in soft green windy hayfields
are left with the sun soaking their souls.
He replenishes the needy and the ones without,
covered in nothing but their skin and the brown mucky dirt of the African sun.
The things us humans have taken from someone that holds all power,
when we have nothing else left,
all we do is ask why when instead we should praise.
His soft white complexion against our soft hands,
because he holds all power and those that deny are given what was taken.
The times when we give up and need help,
when he is waiting to show you his power may come to you and replenish.
For he holds all power and gives back what was taken from those that haven't,
forgiven and forgotten was seemed to be hurting them.
The blue-gray skies covering the rain and thunder storms miles away
is what causes me to smile, for I know that his powers are only beginning
and the sun will shine again.

A Piece of Pi
by Gavin Bittenbender

Everyone loves pie!
However,
Does anyone love pi?
Yes!
All mathematicians would certainly agree,
They all are huge fans of the best ever
Number pi.
It is greater than three, yet
It is smaller than four.
e can't compare,
i doesn't even come close,
Root two just lacks the charm carried by
The ratio of a circle's circumference to its diameter.
Out of all the numbers I've seen,
I'd say that pi is the best one of all!

Family
by Cora Mummert

Tender hearts with hugs so sweet
Like cookies on a cookie sheet
Never leaving me to cry
My family's with me by and by
Forever feeling fantastic and free
I'm loved by them and they're loved by me

Winter
by Joseph Kibbie

Winter is cold and harsh.
The snow and wind burns your face and you sink to your waist.
Kids jump up and down, all over town because today is a snow day.
They put on their hats, gloves, chilly chokers, coats, snow pants, and boots
then run outside and find sticky snow, then build snowmen, snow forts, igloos.
They slide till they can't slide no more.
Their parents are surprised to find them not in front of the television.
When the day is done they go inside for cocoa,
and hate that they have to go to school tomorrow.

Invincible vs. Invisible
by Xandra Wishnefsky

Breathe in, breathe out, you are stronger now
Their words of hate are their own mistakes
Move on stay; strong
Take a deep breath; hold it all in
But we're sick of holding it in
Tear down those walls
Watch as they fall
Now we yell, as we rebel
We are not invisible
They can push, they can shove, they can try to yell above
But we refuse to be invisible
We will be invincible
Our coats fly in the wind, they finally give in
The wall in between has fallen at the seams
They now know their sticks and stones hurt as much as those words they throw
They watch as they roll off our shoulders and we are now once again invincible
and will be till the end

Love
by Zachary Gaulin

Love.
It's a curious thing.
It can be the most wonderful thing in the world. It can be your worst nightmare.
It takes you over from the inside out.
You can love it, or you can hate it. There is nothing in between.
It will eat you up, but will it swallow? Or will it spit you out?
There is no way to describe it, and it can be described in every way.
It is an oxymoron. It is a black hole trying to suck itself up into nowhere.
It is an identity crisis. It is everything, and it is nothing.
It is a perception, like time, yet it is as real as the soil we stand on.
It is confusion in its purest form, and it is full of absolutes.
You can make it, and it can break you.
You can run, and it will hide.
It is a living emotion.
It is fearless courage, and it is fear.
It is happiness, and it is miserable sadness.
It is anger, and it is forgiveness.
It is hatred,
and it is
LOVE

Dreams Come True
by Nikos Stylios

People ask what do I want to be.
I say being a sports player is my dream.
They tell me dreams mostly do not come true.
And that to be a sports player there is a lot to do.
But I know in my heart that sports is for me.
Sports will be my career, that is my dream.
Dreams really do come true, just ignore the haters.
But you know what they say, haters gotta hate.
But sooner or later I will be on the court or the field wearing number 8!
I know that in sports, for the people that make it, there is only a few.
But I know in my heart my dream will come true.

Nature
by Nicholas Fitzsimmons

Nature changes a lot
We change it,
We help it,
We hurt it,
Nature always changes

Autumn Leaves
by Tor Petrov

Autumn leaves fall
Swirling with the wind
rustling, whispering
Telling us of places they have been
Like memories of where we came from
their dry husks slip through our fingers
Ghosts of friends we never knew
how hard these leaves worked, to be cast aside,
like worn through gloves
I must follow them, along the swirl of rolling wind
All I ask is that
You
Remember
Me

Where I'm From
by Christina Duong

I am from dishrags,
And dust bunnies,
From a pair of moldy flip flops that occupied me through the years.
I am from a straw house,
That sheltered ten,
From a place where food was scarce,
And a chicken meant a family feast for days.
I am from a place where it was rare to have more than six outfits a year,
Where school meant money,
Nowhere to be found,
And where a bike had shown you're wealthy.
I am in a Steinbeck tale,
Until the curse is broken,
And when that day comes, I'll be waiting.

If the First Time
by Emilee Clarke

If the first time a boy says "I love you"
is when his fingers are halfway done unbuttoning your favorite blouse, walk away.
You do not have to be naked to be loved.
Your skin does not equate to your heart
and you are not designed to satisfy someone's hunger for flesh.
If the first time a boy says "I love you"
is between shots of vodka, and he ignores you the morning after, do not wait for
him to sober up, walk away. Although drunk minds speak sober thoughts,
you do not have to be with someone who is ashamed to love you
that they can only profess these confessions through the mask of intoxication.
If the first time a boy says "I love you"
is strung between tears, as he drowns himself in the corners of his mind
and drowns his skin in blood, walk away.
Anyone who is stuck in the dark will want to cling to any bit of light,
and you are not built just to be someone's anchor from a storm.
You are not made for lust, disguised under the face of love.
You must not feel obligated to love the boys who say they love you,
if they don't really mean it.
You are not made to live for drunken texts and shameful tones
just because you want someone's hand to hold.
You are not made to be a settler, darling,
don't you dare let yourself be one.

Dreams
by Michael Smith

Dreams can be special
They are about good moments
Never leave a dream

The Hero
by Katelyn Pastir

One day when I stumbled across him
He was broken, beaten, and worn.
He was no longer the strong man I remembered.
He was the man who tried to save the world,
And he was the man who died trying.
A hero in the eyes of some,
A failure in the eyes of others.
A war torn man, who fought no war but his own.
A man, who shall be remembered with honor.
A man, a hunter, a doctor, a genius, a father.
A Hero.

Beloved Sister
by Anna Shaver

All our lives we had each other
laughed, cried, yelled, and even lied.
Another thing I'm not so blind to see
how much you are like me.
I try so hard to set good examples
Sometimes I even make mistakes.
I know life isn't easy
Even when it's not. I will guide you.
When I'm stuck between choices
I wonder how much it will affect you.
Now I know how careful I must be
Taking the wrong road instead of the right.
Most of all, I want you to know
No matter where I am, what I'm doing
Or even who I am with
If you are in trouble, I'll drop everything,
Just to give you my advice.
There will never be an end
What we share together will never die.

The Tree
by Nicholas Deblois

I listen to the wind
telling of summer's end
mixed with the stories of the great old trees
telling of wonderful sights they see
My leaves shiver at the thoughts
of the nights to come,
for I'm only a year old sapling you see
the others do not guide me,
I do not know
what will the snow do to me?
Will it hurt my beautiful little green-as-grass branches?
My arms aching and being weighted down,
My older friends say they were not hurt
but I see the scars left by the past
the wounds covered in sticky sap
they say it was the bear or the woodpecker
but I am a smart young tree
The next day I hear groans and cries
for the day has come
winter has arrived.

The Mighty Ocean
by Asher Solnit

Who are you, to ask me my story?
I am more powerful than you think.
My unexplored depths remain untouched.
You have only seen my insignificant ripples.
You call these weak, worthless events waves and tsunamis,
but there is more to me.
Much more.
I am as deep as thought.
I have the power to nurture the largest of animals and the smallest of them.
I am where life began, but I can also end it.
My long arms can reach far into your home, so don't anger me,
or I shall brew a great storm to wipe you away as you would step on an anthill.
So you see,
I should be respected, but not feared.
I am the mighty Ocean.

In a Far Away Land
by John Bullock

In a far away land deep in outer space,
In a far away land there lived a king and a queen.
In a far away land there is a great castle with huge walls and turrets.
In a far away land there is a great beast that guards the great castle.
In a far away land there is a great knight, who serves the king.
In a far away land there are thousands of people, just like the knight.
In a far away land the people are kind and don't fight.
They live happily together and care for each other.
In a far away land and a very nice place, there's a leader that rules
with a fist of kindness and a brilliant mind.
In a far away land the people are happy and carefree.
That land will be Earth one day,
Let's cherish this freedom all day.

The Man and the Pipe
by Camille Kurtz

Wisps of smoke trace a path through the air
Wistfully climbing into the gray clouds
Chairs stacked lonesomely, collecting coats of dust
On a street corner basking in the fading light
The puff of the pipe and the slow burn of embers creating a glow
Abandonment rings loud, disappointment echoes
He sits, stewing, puffing
Coat pockets nonexistent with the abundance of holes
And the patches on his shoes wear thin
He shares the woeful tune with the rats
Learning each tail and each whisker
Even the stones
The street stones
They wear away and crumble beneath his feet
And all the while the ashes fall
Like flakes of snow, building upon the ground
Light is gone, now
Leaving only the steady burn and rising plume of smoke
As a comfort amidst the night

Sonnet of a Bedroom
by Sam Needleman

The end of hall by splendid books abound,
Magritte, Gauguin; they stack to live a life.
Will record players give my Ella sound,
Convey Simone in all her civil strife?
The wall speaks too: remembrance, primary,
"My Daughter," red to white to black to her,
The aura glum; the presence doesn't try.
She hangs in three, immersed in all allure.
Hermes two thousand, helot under mint,
'Neath portraits. "Kiss," the message vivid clear,
Imposed upon us, portrait blocks by Klimt.
For parts awry, in Avignon we fear.
The books align, collections by and by,
A struggle here, for scratches gone to die.

The Song We Hum
by Catherine O'Keeffe

Saying goodbye, it couldn't be long,
I started to hum, and sing the song.
She said we'd meet again, it wasn't forever,
She wiped my tears, and then said never.
I was only six, and didn't understand,
We were people too, and this was our land.
They came for us loudly, in the night,
It was terrorizing, and a horrid sight.
I packed silently, and all alone,
We might have hid, if we had known.
Screams and demands, I could now hear,
I heard an engine, it was growing near.
A girl younger than I, already in the car,
It started moving, hoping we wouldn't go far.
Shouting and people, were filling the road,
I watched my house vanish, and the life I had known.
She gave me a hug, humming the song too,
I didn't know what was happening, but she perhaps knew.
That was the last time, that I saw my mom,
I was now determined to live, smart and calm.

Summer
by Erin Collins

Early morning, birds chirping, sun rising.
I am running through the dewy grasses.
Hot, lazy days and adventures await.
Days at the beach are my favorite ones,
coconut scented lotion fills the air,
icy cold dips in the salty ocean.
Ice cream melting in the warm summer sun.
Picnic lunches with good friends by the lake,
hot dogs with chips and homemade lemonade.
Warm nights chasing flickering fireflies,
up all night sitting by the cozy fire,
listening to the chirping of crickets.
The warm summer breeze rustles upon leaves.
Wishing upon stars, enjoying summer.

Siblings of Night
by Lilah Bojanoski

I am no one
Nobody knows me, nobody cares
I am alone
Millions of miles from others
Alone in the darkness of night
I could be noticed if I wanted to be
I could be visible in the light of day
I look down upon you, but you never notice
Only few have ever dared question me ...
Us
I am alone,
But we, *we* are light
My brothers and sisters and I
We make your sky magnificent,
Forming heroes and monsters
You've only dreamed of
We are diamonds against the black velvet of night
We are one
We are stars

Our Stars
by Malika Maynard

I want to pretend
we are stars
and I'm simply burning up
but stars are beautiful
and I'm fading faster
than light was meant
to touch shiny
cheeks on dark nights
wrapped in warm hands
and feeling unsafe
like the lonely people
hiding from invisible monsters
who wish
they were just stars

Broken
by Brittney Zimmer

The chilled breeze hits the top of my tingling fingertips
The sun beats down on the burning red ground
Shattered into a thousand pieces, I sit hurting
Letting the time slip by every second I stay
Like an hourglass dropping each tiny piece of sand
Carefully into its perfect place
My broken heart grieves for happiness
As it lays peacefully inside my broken body
Blurred windows make it hard to see the outside world
I feel trapped in a sorrow filled room
Searching for the glue to attach the broken pieces,
That never seem to show its identity
I'm lost in a world that's too big for a girl like me
I push my hand forward
Reaching for help that never seems to come
My hopeful hand stays waiting
Waiting for the piece reaching back to touch the frozen fingers
But will it ever come close enough for me to gain back?
Or will I be broken forever?

3rd Place

Emily Kosker

The Battle (A Dedication To My Mother)
by Emily Kosker

She enters the ring ready to fight
The battle will be tough, but she has God on her side
Determined and ready she gives the first swing
And with a powerful blow she knocks it down
But it bounces back up; it hits her hard
She stumbles a moment but doesn't quit
Though tired and weary, she battles on
A warrior against a cancerous foe
She fights for her family; she fights for her life
We, the spectators, are all on her side
Looking at me, she gives a fearless wink
Then summoning all that's left of her strength
There it is; the knockout blow;
This one is just for me

2nd Place

Olivia Loehr

Abuelo
by Olivia Loehr

My hands move across the lines of yours, young on old, soft on scarred
I know these hands, they've played 'go-fish' and bandaged knobby knees
I know these hands, but I never really knew,
how these hands carried a young man's dreams
how they trembled when your father yelled,
as you hid them in the pockets of your jeans
how the ring threatened to slip from your moist palms
as you bent down on one knee
how your fingers shook as you held your daughter for the first time
how the sun beat down upon your back as you lay the bricks, to make a home
Every crease of your skin shows the strength it took to build a home,
to stay, and the courage summoned to leave, leave it all behind
To bury your broken dreams with the dirt of the land you loved
To begin again in a place of new language and new labels.
These hands, picking your pride off the ground
Scrubbing floors and painting walls
These hands carrying dreams, for your children, of your children
My hands, so small, so frail, rest in yours, so strong, so still
I hold this legacy, I hold my dreams,
hands full with the promise of what waits for me

1st
Place

Veronica Enierga

Employing vivid imagery,
Veronica wrote "Evolution" while in the 9th grade.
Having moved to the United States when she was just four years old,
Veronica has become an accomplished writer,
and continues to sharpen her skills now at the high school level,
where she takes classes in 2D visual arts and theater.
Congratulations on an excellent poem.

Evolution
by Veronica Enierga

She was built upon concrete, compacted sand
The gilded metropolis with all its secrets hidden within flashing lights
Look stark naked to the penetrating eye,
Perversity, lingered in the dark alleys
smelling like must and lust alike, the similarities
It lingered, the heavy perfumes that covered the city
Blocking God's golden whips of fire that burned the clothes right off her,
Leaving her bare to stand before judgment, like Eve and Pandora before her
She let her streets run rampant, as if willingly, seducingly
Letting the poisons she calls wings burn through her veins,
charring her to her roots
Now she stands in rubble, grotesque disfigured glass
No angels guard her gates of entrance, but all leave willingly
Alone, the metropolis cried
displaying her atrocities to purify under the golden sun-
It was instant, leaving nothing but ash and dust in her place
Simply she disappeared, as if Death had not kissed her
but consumed her with all her sins
Leaving nothing to grow but a single blooming 'shroom,
Gray, standing for nothing but for humanity in its most savage form.
Lying in dust she dreams, once she stood on concrete–

Division IV

Grades 10-12

The One
by Garrett Wagner

Be my love
My love for life
Lifelong gift from above
Above created my one day wife
Wife more beautiful than Aphrodite
Aphrodite jealous of her golden locks
Golden locks to compliment eyes as blue as the sea
The sea, not as vast as her knowledge, cunning as a fox
A fox fierce and playful just as much as her towards me
Me, I alone want her to be my love.

I Dislike Poetry
by Maya English

There is neither,
Rhyme nor reason,
Like the weather of this season.
Most of them are angsty,
Or else really sappy,
And I can't really tell
If they're pontificating or crappy
It doesn't make sense,
Except for a few
Pie.

If You Want To Know Me
by Joseph Thompson

If you really want to know me, then think of that chubby kid
That sits in the corner during class, and barely talks to anyone
Think of that shy kid that wears glasses and has a weird haircut
Who always wears nice clothes like jeans and a polo
And expects people to like him more because he is
Or you can think of the fat guy in gym class who tries to fit in
But fails miserably
You can even think of that nice guy who tries to help everyone
And succeeds but isn't even noticed
Either way you think of me, I'm fine with it because, that is me

Looking Back Now
by Brooke Gushanas

Somewhere between white sheets
There is still an us
I wonder if you ever think of me
When you cannot fall asleep at night
Because for me, you're alive in my dreams
It brings the past back to life
And it wakes me with a cold sweat
Because when I look down
At the spaces between my fingers
I can still feel the way your hands
Used to lace with mine
I can still smell your cologne
And see the smile you always wore
That was directed at me
But now all I can think of is how
You were smiling at her
But tell me, dear
Do you ever think of me?

Under the Skin
by Danielle Hann

Love is a word
I feel we should embrace
Some people see it
And it makes their hearts race
They don't look past the walls
Or deeper into the skin
They only see the outside
Instead of what's in
The harder they peer
The more they begin to judge
But the outside they look at
Is merely a smudge
Of the person they're criticizing
Or what they see that exists
But if you do not look hard enough
There is so much more that you'll miss
So if love is a word
We all should embrace
Then we should look past our judgments
And look past the face.

New York City
by Mattia Krappa

My favorite time of the day is night when I'm as alive as New York City
And thoughts of you rush through my mind like people in a hurry to catch a cab.
Thinking of your smile makes my heartbeat race like an underground subway.
I think of everything you've ever said to me, your words like a perfect harmony
erupting from the Radio City stage.
I think of how being away from you for even the smallest amount of time
Makes me feel like a child lost in the big city.
I think of the nights we spend together and how it seems like the world
And everything around just stops and is silent.
With your eyes bright like the lights that decorate Times Square and lips pink
like a rose, I am mesmerized like that same child who is lost in the city.
This child doesn't seem to care, however, because her surroundings are beautiful
and bright like you at any given time or day.
Maybe that's what I think about most;
No matter how rough or easy my life seems to be,
My favorite place like my favorite city takes me from my reality.
I am the child hopelessly lost in the city and my city is you.

Let Me Out
by Alexa Reidenauer

This isn't Wonderland anymore
This stuff is in her soul
Always loud, never silent
She pushes them away
They steal the song she used to sing
The memories morph into unidentifiable creatures
They take the form of everything she's lost
Always loud, never silent
This stuff has stolen everything familiar
When did this happen?
She can't remember the before, only the after
They encircle her, always
Entangled in her soul
She let them in, she wants them out
Her feet, they kick
Her hands, they push
Who is she?
This is her new destiny
They entered her soul and forever changed her world
Always loud, never silent

Ocean Ties
by Brandiwyne Walus

Oh no, there brews a storm out in the seas
Portside, starboard, bow, stern – round the ships turn
The waves coming forth are taller than trees
Hurricane rain with the wind makes our eyes burn
Don't fret not just yet, this happened before
Bond together, be stronger than this storm
Nature's way making sure life's not a bore
Mother Earth decided she needs new form
Now lightning, come on, scary as can be
Saying my prayers to ease the worry
It's working, I hear a mermaid sing to me
When it's over go see what is buried
Lightning hit the beach and shiny I see
Shiny glass orbs in the sand, how can that be?

The Heart That Has Bled
by Caitlyn Olszewski

To escape my mind; that would be the ultimate escape.
To free myself from this world and all the pain that it carries.
Pain that will break me, pain that will make me
But pain nevertheless.
The continuous flashes of the past;
The unconquerable tears that stream from my eyes
That only come alive in the dark in the dead of the night
When no one can hear.
When will the suffering end?
When will the light reach towards me and take my heart and make it whole again?
The burden does not leave.
It burns with a fire that is ignited again
Every time the memories visit me.
Visiting hours are coming to a close.
I am letting go of the dark past that haunts me.
No longer will it have a hold on my heart.
My time will come and the light will embrace me
And a smile will mean much more
than a simple expression of temporary happiness.
It will be infinite; my heart will be infinite.
Long live the heart that has bled.

I Am
by Alyssa Bostany

I am like a butterfly,
Floating carelessly in the wind,
Providing beauty and serenity,
Portraying freedom through my wings.
I am like a cloud,
Wandering aimlessly throughout the sky,
Changing shape and direction,
Thunderstorming when I cry.
I am like light,
Helping some find their way,
Providing visibility,
Warning darkness to stay away.
I am like a song,
Echoing throughout the room,
Enlightening those who listen,
Instilling a catchy tune.

The Astronaut
by Adam Capuano

Floating in the black abyss,
The unknown surrounding him from every angle,
Air gone with any other life; devoured by claustrophobia.
Alone in the emptiness with only thoughts,
Sucked in by submissive forces of the superior planets,
While attached to the mothership,
An ongoing battle rages on around him.
Dodging asteroids left and right,
Silence creeping through the voice inside his head.
His conscience echoing throughout his brain,
Vibrant nebulas splashing the abyss.
Paralyzed by fear, driven by curiosity,
Yet welcomed by freedom,
He claws for fast arriving future.
Breaking ties with the ship,
Pushing past the planets and asteroids.
He reaches for new stars, stopping at each one.
Endlessly drifting until he reaches his last star– his last nebula.
He is the astronaut.
We are astronauts.

If You're Mine
by John Lorenzon

I'll be there through the ups and downs,
No matter smile or frown
My trust will forever be yours,
If you'll be mind to adore
Be my one and only,
Together we'll never be lonely
Forever give you my heart,
Let this be just the start.

Dancer
by Lely Le

I am a 16 year old girl that weighs approximately 115 pounds
and is five feet and one inch tall. I do not have long legs nor a long torso.
My clothing consists of baggy pants, a muscle tank and sneakers.
And hey guess what, I'm a dancer.
No, I do not dance hip hop although my apparel would like to contradict me.
My feet move along the stage ever so lightly
and with every leap I can reach the stars.
From every fall out of a pirouette comes new bruises
that then become my version of battle scars.
On the floor I am anyone I may please, a soldier even
because with every battle won an even bigger war approaches.
Dancing contemporary is not just another style of dance
it's a way of being in the clouds and still remaining on solid ground
it's a cloak that binds me keeping me safe and sound.
Dance is my version of flying seeing as I'm afraid of heights
even though it seems that when I take the stage I'm on a roller coaster ride
with my slippers by my side there is no type of dance that I cannot do.
Ballet, salsa, tango, waltz, swing, bachata, merengue, contemporary,
and yes even hip hop, I am guilty for dancing all of the above
because I do not say no to something that I love, and I love to dance.
Although I do not belong to any fancy studio, I still continue to practice
and even when fail I know I have won, because I have a growing mind.
My mind allows my body and my soul to connect
and to make the perfect mistakes so that I can learn.
I am a 16 year old girl that weighs approximately 115 pounds
and is five feet and one inch tall, I may not have the perfect dancer's body but,
I AM A DANCER.

Football
by Jerry Hobbs

There once was a game called football
where the players knew how to trip and fall.
They were clumsy it's true
you see they wore panther's blue
and the coach never knew what to call

Smile
by Vanessa Blose

What's in a smile?
A silent "Hello"
An "I believe you"
"I'm proud of you"
A word before you go
What's in a smile?
A "you've got a friend in me"
An "I love you"
"I trust you"
A "go and be free"

I Wonder Why We Said Our Goodbyes
by JJ Roberts

I wonder why you left us so soon,
kind of surprised and out of the blue,
I know you've been hurting the past couple years,
every time I think of your struggle, it brings me to tears,
You fought and you fought, till your very last day,
giving some kinds of hope in indecisive ways,
I didn't leave your side for those awful six days,
hiding my sorrows as much as I may,
We knew it would happen, just didn't know when,
the doctor said he couldn't tell just then,
It was that awful Tuesday morning as I watched you slip away,
holding on tighter in hope to make you to stay,
I miss you so much, you don't even know,
the struggle I have is painful and slow,
The days have gone by, a month slipped away,
still thinking you're here and only a phone call away,
You are finally with your one true love,
Nana, I know you're watching above.

Falling
by Bettina Cambridge

Falling in mid-air
Through and through
Down I drop, down I drop, I fall
Looking for a wall to grab
I can't breathe, engulfed in nothing
Screaming help, save me
Lost, can't see my way out of the darkness
Exit, there's no exit
Slowly my body turns frigid
Down I drop into the hole
Slipping, slipping away
Falling in mid-air
Through and through
Down I drop, down I drop, I fall
Gone.

Love Poem
by Sianni Cubbage

True love is hard to find
When you find love it makes you blind
The only thing around, is you and me
Being with you makes me feel free
When you find love it makes you blind
My love, he is always in my mind
Being with you makes me feel free
When I'm with you it's hard for me to see
My love, he is always in my mind
But, then you hurt me over time
When I'm with you it's hard for me to see
How much pain that you gave to me
But, then you hurt me over time
Our love was like a crime
How much pain that you gave to me
Why did you hurt me?
Our love was like a crime
You were such a slime
Why did you hurt me?
True love is hard to find

Empty Parking Lot Thoughts
by JadenLee Watkins

Chains are overused,
Oh, these misery blues,
A heavy pair of shoes,
And a fuse,
What a troubling night,
This is no sight,
Heavy rocks upon my chest,
I just wish this gnawing would rest,
A mind that races,
It does not matter the place,
Needing some peace,
I forget how to breathe,
My lungs were seized,
Like I was drowning,
It is more than a frown,
This anxiety,
I slightly enjoy this troubled society,
Like a swing,
I go down and go up,
I must be a king of this crazy domain.

Change
by Dana Pollock

What about change makes us so uncomfortable?
is it because we've fallen into a pattern and it is being broken?
change is not always negative, but it is often viewed as so.
when something, anything, changes, it leaves opportunity to reminisce on the past,
and ponder what could have been if things stayed the same.
when things change, it leaves an awful amount of uncertainty
for the future and what it holds.
sometimes change is so drastic that nothing is ever the same again,
for the good or the bad.
sometimes it is so minuscule that no one even notices.
change provides growth for those who are leaving the bad behind.
change can make a hermit crawl out of their shell, or further in.
the point is, change can either be good or bad and most of the time
there is nothing we or anyone can do to prevent change, it just happens.
that's what makes change funny;
it has a mind of its own and is only looking out for itself;
we just have to learn to suck it up, and go with it.

Fate
by Angela Callery

Fate never handed me anything.
I did not unwrap a present of strength.
I did not pull from a bag, my courage.
My happiness did not come with a bow around it.
Everything I have, I had to work for.
My forgiveness did not come brand new.
It was dented from being tossed around in a sea of hate,
Crashing against many jagged rocks.
The endurance I have, I was not born with.
It was a long run to build it,
With many injuries and hills along the way.
There are many who just had life handed to them,
With high quality products.
But in the end, I'm happy I worked for mine.

The Dying Ember
by Andrew Nosti

There is a land endowed with liberty
In which all people are born equal.
But is every man and woman truly free
Or does that land still consider some people
To be less worthy than all the others?
This nation was born of men who fought tyranny
Yet those fathers allowed it to be legal
To strip an entire race of its dignity.
It took a war to end these medieval
Practices and for two races to live as brothers.
Then after six score and ten years of being
Second class citizens, women were forever
Assured suffrage, in turn guaranteeing
The ability to vote despite gender,
Securing another victory in equal rights.
Now this great nation is finally agreeing
To stamp out the last, dying ember
In the fire of injustice, freeing
The right of marriage to every member.
Thus ending the last of its immoral plights.

Youth Is Our Adventure
by Laura Jean Null

There's this place few people go,
by the docks not many know,
sneak away on an adventure,
being young and wild just to venture.
We are making history that will never repeat itself,
the odd part is in 20 years we will still be ourselves.
Escaping the world and living it up forever,
the moments of youth we will always remember.
We'll infinitely make mistakes and learn,
as of now, we'll have that constant firing passion in our hearts that will burn.
A couple of years from now, high school won't matter,
society's standards are lifted so high just to flatter.
As for right now though,
we'll sit on these docks,
not wasting precious time counting clocks.

Going Away To College
by Marissa Kowalski

Your rough callused hands caressed my face for the last time.
Hundreds of miles away.
The reality sets in that in two short hours you'll no longer be mine.
Lost to the many new experiences that life will afford you.
How could you leave me? Why is our young love forbidden?
You are my Romeo and Boston University is the Capulets
stealing you away from me.
Life has slapped me in the face with the hand of the future.
Forced to choose what you'll be for the rest of your life ... without me.
One hundred fears run red and rampant across my face and,
although you say this is not the end, a scarlet letter glows on your chest.
How will you stay faithful to me?
How will you fend off the forbidden fruit?
Why won't you stay?
Tears run hard down my face and you pick up my chin and tell me good-bye.
A dagger sinks deep through my chest.
My mother tells me I'm too young to cry for a boy.
If she only knew the fear and hate and love and loss I felt all at one time.
Time heals every wound.
So did Thanksgiving break, when I saw your face for the first time in months;
although the beard was a new touch.

Under the Snow
by Shauna Martel

Pale white fingers, as cold as ice
Forgotten souls roaming the night
All seem dead, but somehow alive
Trying to find their meaning inside
Roaming the streets under the pale moonlight
Those souls searching, searching for what is right
Shining bright with that unearthly sheen
Stuck in the world of in-between
Crying their sad melodies of their broken heart
Left in the dark unable to part
Flowers forever falling on their graves,
The beautiful red petals shrivel and die
With every year that's passing by.
All the sadness, that constant sadness
Shown wherever those souls go
Their lives cut short under that evening snow.

Creative Debris
by Kaila Shields

We all start out as inexperienced painters to a blank canvas,
Picture painting for the blind and storytelling to the deaf.
We strive for the impossible to become possible again,
Praying to the omnipotent for the ability to wield creativity once more,
Dancing like jobless fools on the boulevard, drunk off the taste of bitter love.
We are not trapped but held captive by the most terrifying of all things; the mind.
It is the mind telling us harming ourselves is a solution to dealing with our pain.
It is the mind knowing the difference between right and wrong
and still holding apathy toward the consequences.
It is the mind carving inspiration into our souls to imprint onto the margins
of our notebooks during class.
It is the mind giving us clusters of scrambled words to create poetic beauties.
It is the mind giving us a dream to dream.
It has always been the mind.
So prove it to them.
Become the definition of what they strive to be.
Let these walls of your precious mind burst open so far that there are no longer
any boundaries to create around the debris of the rubbled creativity.
Just write something today because even if it sucks,
Someone will think it's beautiful.

Perfect
by Elizabeth Curless

Perfect is a picture, an image, a photograph.
Perfect is 120 soaking wet, and 5'6" achieved with heels,
Hairspray, love and smiles– always look perfect
So no one sees when you're not.
Perfect is small talk– telling the world about your future
And making something up so it looks like you have one.
To be perfect is to live and love.
To be perfect is to be happy.
Perfect is a picture,
Fallen from a wallet, fallen from a pile.
Perfect is silence because your words are unwanted.
It's burying anger and sadness inside you, so no one can see what perfect really is.
To be perfect is to hurt and to starve.
To be perfect is to be alone.
Perfect is falling from the grace of the world.
To be perfect is to die.
Perfect is a picture on fire,
It begins beautiful,
And slowly chars
Into nothingness.

Brown Eyes
by Tia Farmer

You see those brown eyes
Aren't they beautiful?
So dark and lovely
But if you look long and hard enough
Maybe you'll see the pain,
The hurt, the low self-esteem,
The depression, the craziness.
The yearning feeling to be someone
To be seen, to be known, to be heard.
You see those brown eyes
Did you know just last night
They cried themselves to sleep
That they looked in the mirror and hated what they saw?
No, because you never
Truly look into someone's eyes
But if you look deep enough
You'll see all these things
Behind my
Brown eyes.

Without Her
by Bri Lewis

Without her
nails clicking on the hardwood floor
and tags jingling while she walks
The house feels so quiet
Without her
beds lying in every room
and toys scattered across the floor
The house feels so empty
Without her
warm body pressed into mine
and tongue licking my cheek
I feel so alone

Memory List Poem
by Sabrina Perri

I opened Italy and all my memories poured out
I remember almost drowning in the sea and my entire family watched
from the shady umbrellas but luckily my dad saved me
that was the day I learned how to swim
I remember when Nonno took us to the store to buy the biggest watermelon ever
I remember peeing in the woods during a picnic
because god forbid some one install a portable bathroom
You gotta do what you gotta do
I remember the time I got the stomach flu
and Aunt Stella force-fed me the next day with sweets and soup
no one could ever go hungry in her presence
I remember visiting my other grandpop's grave, shockingly I didn't cry
I remember getting propelled on the beach by the biggest wave I've ever seen
I remember giving Nonna Giovanna soup since she was bedridden
her smile lingers in my mind
I remember ordering food for the first time in Italian, "Voglio la pizza"
I remember being scared in the gondola in Venice
because the weight did not seem to be proportional
and plotting how far I must swim in case it tipped over
I remember every time seeing Uncle Mario with his crooked neck
and perfect English asking my dad for twenty bucks and some cigarettes
I remember saying goodbye to Nonna Santina and Aunt Stella
they made me feel so guilty
I oppressed my memories back once again and dealt with my surroundings.

The Busy Animals
by Erika Licciardone

Fred the Frog frolicked through the forest for fourteen flies.
Silly Sarah the Squirrel sat and sang sappy songs about spring.
Billy the Bobcat blew a billion bubbles.
Ted the Turtle told the time by touching his toes twice.
Rosie the Raven rambunctiously ravaged a rat.
Wendy the Wolf whistled while walking by the water wonderfully.
The adventurous animals all had joyful fun in the forest.

Fast Forward
by Diane Pak

Today starts out with 86,400 seconds in a day.
How on Earth we pass this day and the day after that, then so on this whole year.
People who walk by every day doesn't even bother to say Hi
People who talk to each other maybe doesn't have time to have a conversation.
People who love each other have secrets, wanting to tell to love ones
doesn't have a whole life to actually open up to.
People who have difficult lives can be hard at first but they will follow each day
but as other why can they live if they can't live a moment
by 84,000 seconds in a day.
What if people realize that love at first sight isn't real of theirs,
which create even happier moment to make things better.
When trying to re-kindle the flying sparks gift.
People argue, people fight why not know the existing part isn't true to even bother.
The elements are Earth, Fire, Water, and Air.
People breathe at living moments to see people grow happy and love
and they say that "the absences makes the heart grow fonder."
What if love is honest and as William Shakespeare say, "that love maybe blind."
We are given subjects at school and the next day it's a new beginning.
We are once told "I Love You" but what if it doesn't it make sense
if the other person broke that saying.
We are called humans.
We get upset, cry. Laugh, and be just happy.
It doesn't makes sense when we live fast forward.
When it comes to mind that it was just a second and then 59 seconds,
then 60 seconds, which is a whole minute.

Love's Slobbering Demise
by Olivia Christman

Love is like a dog with a bone.
The dog drops the bone at your feet, an invitation, a plea, a question.
You pick up the bone, love springs up like the dog,
Catching the bone in mid-air. Elation explodes.
Then slowly descends. He trots back.
The bone is now displeasing, dripping with goo.
You're only willing to sacrifice two fingers.
The throw suffers, weak, disappointing.
But the dog still goes, isn't bothered. Too infatuated to notice.
Brings it back tail wagging.
The bone drenched, with a strand or two of grass set in slobber.
The same two fingers. The same disheartened throw.
The dog still pleased, notices something.
The bone spit out at your feet, a different question.
Can it fly as it did before? Can you fix it? Can we continue to play?
But the bone is spotted, oozing brown-green pieces. It's no longer worth it.
The dog's joy is not worth your sacrifice. It's not worth getting your hands dirty.
It doesn't make you happy anymore. You turn, leave.
The dog tied to the tree with the bone where your feet used to be.

Darkness Comes, the Demons Follow
by Jourdan Aten

Whispered screams slither through the night, closer and closer they come.
So very close that I can decipher their strangled words.
The demons the screams originate from, giggle as their words
slowly twist around my body, chaining me to my bed.
The chains grow tighter and tighter with every breath,
until the breath comes out as shattered gasps.
They laugh as their words slink into my thoughts,
and soon even those are contorted.
My thoughts become as dark as the night that surrounds me.
The room grows colder and colder, until I feel my very heart freeze in place.
My screams are snatched by the demons, and they snicker at my pain.
They grin as their whispers become sharpened.
Their smiles grow wider as the sharp whispers caress my skin.
They kiss the tears from my cheeks, still laughing.
I can hear it, their laughter, even after the sunlight drives them away.
Even after my heart is no longer still,
no longer surrounded by the freezing darkness.
Even after my thoughts are my own once more.
Deep somewhere in the crevices of the most shadowy part of my mind,
their laughter echoes, dancing with their promises to return.

The Waters of Being
by Rachel Brunnquell

I have grasped, found, imagined this light, so eager it flows—
waiting for my plight but scarcely moments after it is found
nothing but darkness seems to be around
I bang and scratch on the door; pound
humming, writhing, I try to fold into myself
desperate attempts to block out the sound
or is it not in noise but silence that I drown?
gurgling through, it flows to the top
pushed, dragged, shuffled through when all I want is to stop
going, going, but not till I'm gone— just till I drop
somehow not gone yet appearing to be lost
lost amongst all too much familiarity, yet they all seem blinded by clarity
the lesser disgraced, as long as you have a pretty face
it's supposed to sweeten the taste
of life, isn't that right?
But the drowning chains of pain
must only bring out the blue in her eyes
the water crashes around the sea
the waves hit the bank harder than lies
twisted torments wearing at her psyche

That's Not a Sport
by Courtney Wuertz

I float around in a pink tutu

I run across the field in my cleats

Most people don't consider what I do a sport

My game is the highlight on Sunday afternoons

We are both athletes

I just want to land that triple pirouette

I need to score a touchdown

I can't let my group down

I have to catch that ball

We are both striving for perfection

If I could just jump a little higher

If I could throw just a little farther

This practice will pay off

We are both athletes

My Brothers
by Jalen Cain

I don't have any friends
I have brothers
The 6
They are my brothers
I have brothers
We always have fun
They are my brothers
There's never a dull moment
We always have fun
We're always together
There's never a dull moment
Always arguing and playing the game
We're always together
Talking about girls
Always arguing and playing the game
We trust each other
Talking about girls
We are a brotherhood
We trust each other
I don't have any friends

I Found the End In Your Eyes
by Emily Haley

By the time the world stopped, we were silent.
There was nothing to counter the sound of our heartbeats hitting asphalt,
of hands fluttering against sides, trying to stretch out to reach to one another,
falling short, so short we can feel the air in the gap between our fingertips.
There is no Heaven.
What was promised to some was not promised to us,
and we found no nirvana, no white gates on clouds, only silence.
Somehow, it seemed to suit us more than any life after life could.

Life
by Kimberly Douma

You want to grow up; but you should make time last.
Life is not forever, it's just a temporary home/place/time.
Do not forget to smile, even if you're sad.
Make friends, but then make new ones.
Fall in love and fall in love again.
Don't forget to sing, even if you're no good.

Priceless
by Camie Yokote

Electrifying gold sparks wrap around my veins and travel into my heart
Jumpstarting a flow of emotions
Sweat beads like drops of dew on a rainy morning
Heat rushes to the skin for everyone to see
Voice a little shaky
Steps quite hesitant
Soon it all fades into a mirage never to appear again
Just
Like
That
It is all over
Steps more dignified
Voice like a Royal
Vivid red encloses a dazzling white
Step out of the light
Into the darkness
But when it is needed
Let it rise
And let the gold come out to play once again

Love Is Everything
by Abigail Christin Jacob

Love works out many problems
Even it is big or little issues
It teaches us a lot of things
Even with heavy sorrowful heart.
Even it is big or little issues
It takes time to understand
Even with heavy sorrowful heart
Love is a solution.
It takes time to understand
Unless you can resolve it
Love is a solution
It changes from old you to new you.
Unless you can resolve it
It does make sense, however
It changes from old you to new you
Love is everything.
It does make sense, however
Love is a choice to choose
Love is everything
Love works out many things.

The Boy Who Showed Me Love
by Audrey Schlais

There was a boy that I once knew,
His face was pale, his eyes a bright blue,
He sits at home in lonely despair,
A young high school boy with bright light brown hair,
The day I met him, he was smiling and jumping,
but I soon came to know his emotions were clumping,
And then for me tragedy struck,
He came to my rescue, I knew I was in luck,
He saved me from death, once, twice, maybe more,
As also to my surprise he opened a new door,
A new world I could see beyond my heartbreak,
My first kiss he gave me, my breath away it did take,
I couldn't say a word, not even a muttered sound,
For deep into that kiss, away my pain had drown,
Yet that had been almost four years ago,
He brought me to life and carried my soul,
To the safety of love, and though we're apart,
We will always have the feeling of love between our hearts.

Art's Relevance
by Erica Lusky

There are no words
To define sempiternal magnificence.
It chooses to express
The views of our ancestors' convictions
Of others and ourselves
That defines us, as a unit
We breathe.
In outrageous styles, it proves
The nonexistence of iniquity.
That remains still, undiscovered.
Between bleeding passion and yearning pain,
It blooms to silence.
To protect us from the weeds of self-depiction
But instead flourishes
Out of our truth, purity, evils, and ability.
Ours hearts, blinded,
Sing with desperate insignificance
When it's entirely undiscovered,
Sleeping, waiting
Upon the sleepless to reveal our symbiotic truth.

Drop of Snow
by Natasha Igl

Slowly am I fashioned together
Collected tears and frozen hearts added to my dress
Stitched together with a careful hand
Blown away by a chilled, departing kiss
Fall from cushy clouds, spun together like cotton
Fellow brothers and sisters tumble down to Earth
"Wait!" I shout, reaching for the slipping sky
No one's left to listen
Collectively we fall, painting verdant hair with broken white bodies
Among a world that reeks of woodsy smoke
Still alive, we weep salty icicle drops
With broken fingers, we cling to each other and everything around us
Together we paint the Earth white

I Won't Let It
by Megan Nashiwa

"Do this, wear that.
You're ugly because you're fat!"
The cruel words that every child hears.
They go so deep that they cause endless tears.
How often does a girl cry herself to sleep?
How many teens commit suicide every week?
Society came up with a formula for what they think you should be,
Even though they tell us to be happy and free.
Thigh gaps do not define beauty– big hearts do.
Protruding hipbones are not pretty, nor are they cool.
That boy uses his sleeve to cover some scars and a stitch.
That girl's frown is where her smile used to sit.
Judgments are the bars that keep our souls locked away,
And these rules that we follow barely get us through the day.
We trap ourselves for thinking these ways are right.
And very few people have the will to fight.
Society is controlling us like an eternal prison,
But we need to teach ourselves, "what is" and "what isn't"
Yes, Society killed that teen,
But I'm not letting Society kill me.

Sky
by Raleigh Leach

The sky
To most, it's just a sky
But to me,
It's as if the great seas were floating
With the clouds as fish
Swimming east or west,
To most the sky is boring
But to me,
It's a painting
That changes every day
Never can it be boring or original
It's a mystery with no key,
But those who call it just a sky
Don't see things the way I see them
Or
They're just boring and old.

Light
by Bridget Murphy

Dusk is nearing.
The flower soaks in the day.
The golden sun–
reflecting on its petals provides life.
It stands tall proudly and hopeful to survive the night to come.
The sun falls beyond the horizon.
Night has taken over.
The cold, lonely night shrouds life–
invites nothing but desolation.
As the flower is alone–
weak and yearning hopeful for day.
As the sun breaks through the darkness,
there is hope.
Sun warms its petals providing life eternal.
The bright fire providing life–
Providing everlasting hope.

Evan Fishburn

Etcetera
by Evan Fishburn

There she is, over there, the one outfitted in the artless gown
made of cotton, and the lace apron made of cambric – see her?
The one with the paperbound book balanced delicately on her knee,
with a good head on her shoulders
and a pristine Bachelors in English framed on her apartment wall?
Yeah, that one, with the wispy white hair and limbs – thin and frail –
and the pallid skin and mellifluous features so delicate
they look sketched on this very afternoon;
the one who wants to write for the – Times
and get swept away by the success of her own anonymity,
and live in the city, and pass the Sunday markets
and buy a parcel of sweet rolls and honeydew
and chrysanthemums (even though she's allergic);
she wants to stroll past the tuileries in April,
wearing those designer shoes by –,
and pose for the flashing cameras in her mind …
See her hands tremble as she turns a page?
And her head turn toward the women entering from across the room?
She isn't like them, tied down to a reputation or a man who sells stocks.
No, she'd rather embark on an expedition of an extravagance worth keeping.
She'd rather be the nameless face, reading, alone,
afraid to lose it all.

2nd Place

Shaloni Pinto

Bombay Slum Evening
by Shaloni Pinto

The old woman sits wobbling the child on her venerable frame.
Her paper hands cover the child's portly fists in a warm embrace
as she croons an age-old lullaby midst the russet red dust coating
the barren roads and the skeleton remains of a town,
now exuberant with hued and crowded tents.
The evening sunset sinks,
trailing the woman's chair and animating her shadows
which fall into haze of angled rubble
and uncharacteristic putrescence that envelops the pair.
The child gazes at the crinkled face of the woman,
warbling in tones only known to harmony of their off-pitch voices.
The blur of daylight
combined with the screaming children and desperate parents
has assuaged to despondence visible
in the yearning looks of the meager children,
who with bones sharply protruding from their bodies,
lay their heads on their mothers laps' dreading the days to come.
The nimbleness of the lullaby seems to escape the constricting air,
the mass of growing shadows, the rubble of an exhausted town
till all who are packed in clusters of weary masses attune their ears to hear
the nearest concept of a foreign notion named
hope.

Brittany Loveless

Every time we read this submission by Brittany,
it reveals something new, something deeper.
It is obvious that this brilliant young author
is passionate about reading and writing
and has spent years perfecting her technique.
An adventurer at heart, Brittany travels whenever she can.
From winter ski trips to summer camping with her three younger sisters,
she just naturally sees the world through the eyes of a writer.
It gives us great pleasure to present
this year's grade 10-12 and Editor's Choice Award winner ...
Brittany Loveless and "Home Alone."

Editor's Choice Award

Home Alone
by Brittany Loveless

Damp wooden planks lie staggered across the floorboard,
bent rusty nails keeping them in place.
she hides in the corner leaning; holding up what's left of the wall,
and it pushes back; holding up what's left of her.
hunched over with her knees molded to her chest,
huge sobs rack her body,
taking over, like an irregular heartbeat.
gripping the picture, she'd do anything to go back to that picture,
that picture, no matter how it makes her mind scream in agony
torn along the edges, the slightly faded image marked in fingerprints,
covers up the deception of an 'All-American' family.
posed ... with quiet smiles plastered onto their silhouettes,
showcasing pearly white teeth, painfully positioned next to each other.
artificial laughter, suspended, in the air, in that moment,
to cover up the hushed lies
that are so clear now that there's nothing else to see.
Strength drained from remembering the nightmare,
she regrets letting the weeds of lies grow out of the picture
and tangle in her reality ... too late, once again.
The fire, thirsting for fuel,
doesn't always get rid of the wood in the process of burning,
but scars it, scorches it, and then pushes it to the side
leaving a smoky reminder of what it never was.

Index
of
Authors

Index of Authors

Index of Authors

Index of Authors

Index of Authors

Accolades
Price List

Initial Copy 32.95

Additional Copies 24.00

Please Enclose $6 Shipping/Handling Each Order

Must specify book title and name of student author

Check or Money Order Payable to:

The America Library of Poetry
P.O. Box 978
Houlton, Maine 04730

Please Allow 4-8 Weeks For Delivery

THE AMERICA
LIBRARY OF POETRY

www.libraryofpoetry.com

Email: generalinquiries@libraryofpoetry.com